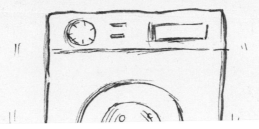

This book should be returned to any branch of the
Lancashire County Library on or before the date

Lancashire County Library
Bowran Street
Preston PR1 2UX

D0363981

Doodlemum

Doodlemum
a year of family life

TWO
ROADS

First published in Great Britain in 2013 by Two Roads

An Hachette UK company

Copyright © John Stevens 2013

The right of A .... has been
asserted by her .... Act 1988.

All rights rese .... reproduced, ... ored in a
retrieval syster ..... or transmitted, in any form or by any means without ..... the prior
written permis .... of the publisher, nor ..... otherwise ..... in a ..... form of
binding or cover other than that in which it is published and without a similar
condition being imposed on the subsequent purchaser.

A CIP catalogue record for this title is available from the British Library

Hardback ISBN 978 1 444 76804 6
eBook ISBN 978 1 444 76805 3

Printed by C&C Printing Offset Co., Ltd., China

Hodder & Stoughton policy is to use papers that are natural, renewable
and recyclable products and made from wood grown in sustainable forests.
The logging and manufacturing processes are expected to conform to the
environmental regulations of the country of origin.

Hodder & Stoughton Ltd
338 Euston Road
London NW1 3BH

www.hodder.co.uk

www.tworoadsbooks.com

LANCASHIRE COUNTY LIBRARY

3011812675607 5	
Askews & Holts	12-Apr-2013
306.850222 STE	£16.99

Doodlemum, the author and illustrator of this book, lives in Swansea with her small zoo of children, animals, washing and sketchbooks. It rains a lot where she lives. She is married to Myles (who would like to be a full time Viking). She likes to drink tea, draw and then drink some more tea.

Doodlemum's real name is Angie Stevens. Angie continues to upload a drawing a day to doodlemum.com.

January

February

May

June

September

October

March

April

July

August

November

December

Welcome

Hello. You've stumbled across my life! Let me tell you something about my family. Probably a lot like yours!

I used to draw a lot, but when my third child Gruff was born, I stopped

So what did I do? I picked up one of the sketchbooks my husband had bought me and I drew aspects of family life that gave me joy...

I started a blog. I called it Doodlemum (well they were only doodles after all). Every night, I would upload a drawing about our day (no matter how mundane or silly it was) and, slowly, the collection of drawings grew. And people seemed to like them, whether they were new parents or 'old hands'. So, I put some of those drawings in this book together with a whole lot of new ones.

Let me introduce the family...

This is Myles, my husband. He loves to cook and
is rather good at it (actually brilliant).

Meet Millie, our eldest daughter.
Millie is a book fiend, budding artist and Doctor·Who fan.

This is Evie, our younger daughter. Evie lives in a world of dinosaurs and fluffy toys. She also needs at least five costume changes a day to satisfy her dressing up urge.

This is Gruff, our youngest son. Gruff loves swords and superheroes. His ambition is to resist knocking down any tower he builds for more than ten seconds.

Our cat called Arnie.
No tail. Only he knows why.

Our dog Bonnie, a gangly,
happy rescue dog with
a bouncy ball obsession.

Our hens and Gizmo, our cockerel.

This book is a collection of the adventures, the ups and downs of family life - the sunny days and the rainy ones. I think it's like all families really - noisy, messy and wonderful. I hope you enjoy A Year of Family Life as much as I have enjoyed living and re-creating it. Perhaps you'll find some familiar moments, from washing baskets and toys to those special family moments. Most of all, I hope you find an opportunity to celebrate family life! It's precious.

Angie Stevens aka Doodlemum

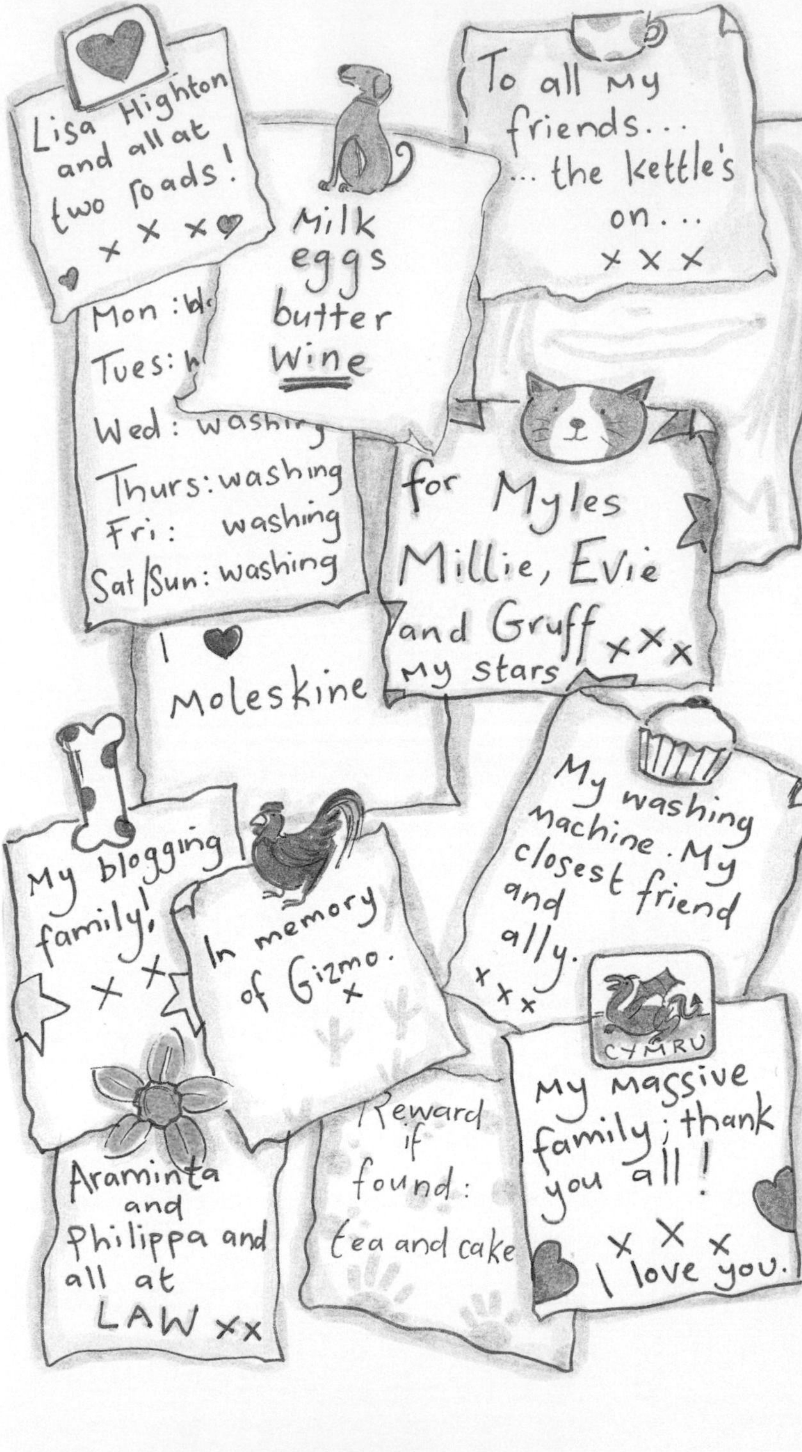
Lisa Highton and all at two roads! x x x
To all my friends... ... the kettle's on... x x x
Milk eggs butter Wine
Mon: wa
Tues: w
Wed: washing
Thurs: washing
Fri: washing
Sat/Sun: washing
for Myles Millie, Evie and Gruff xxx my stars
I ♥ Moleskine
My washing machine. My closest friend and ally. xxx
My blogging family! xx
In memory of Gizmo. x
CYMRU
My massive family; thank you all! xxx I love you.
Araminta and Philippa and all at LAW xx
Reward if found: tea and cake

January

out with the old, in with the new...

Happy New Year, cough cough...

leaving so soon Arnie, that bad here is it?

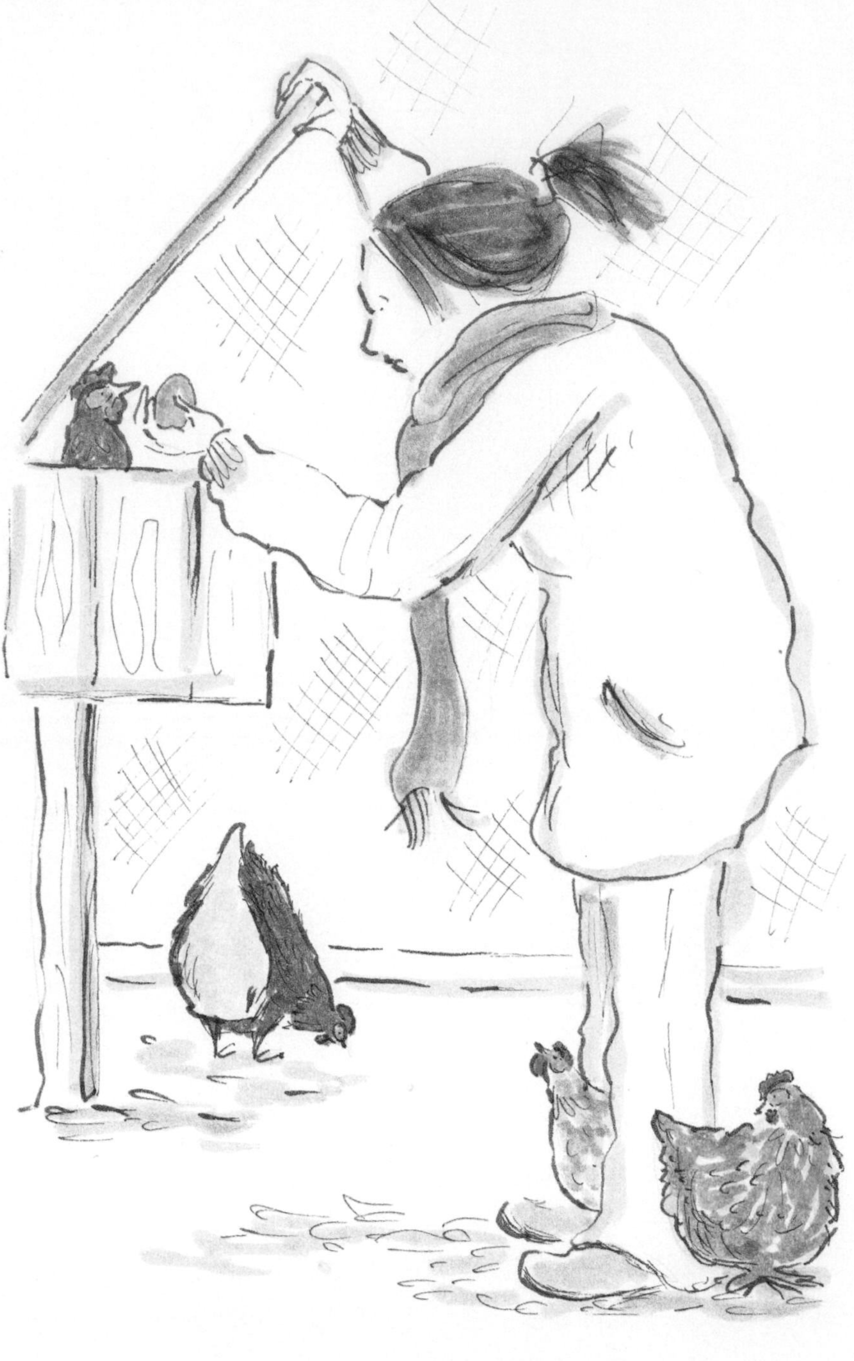

Laying...

...and digging for victory!

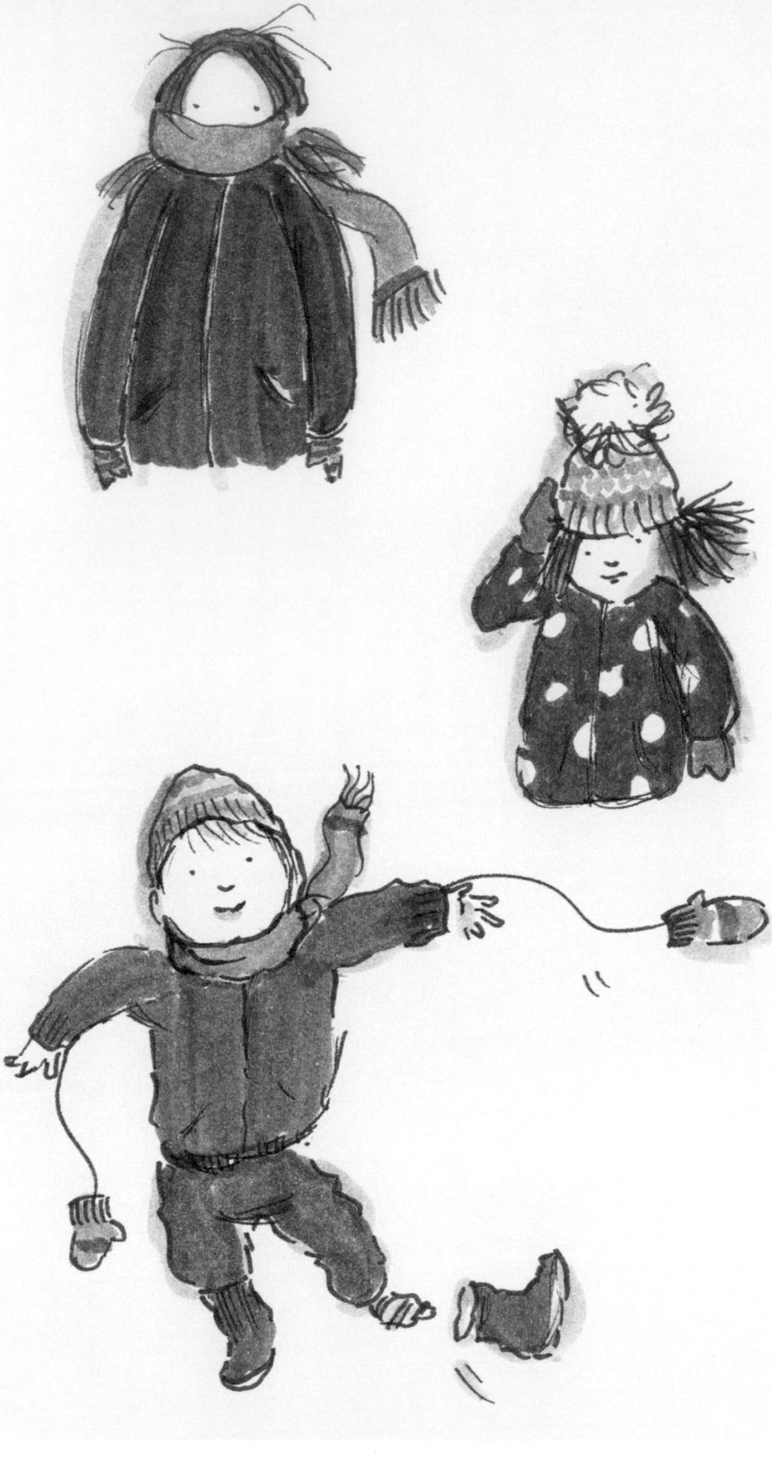

are we warm enough?

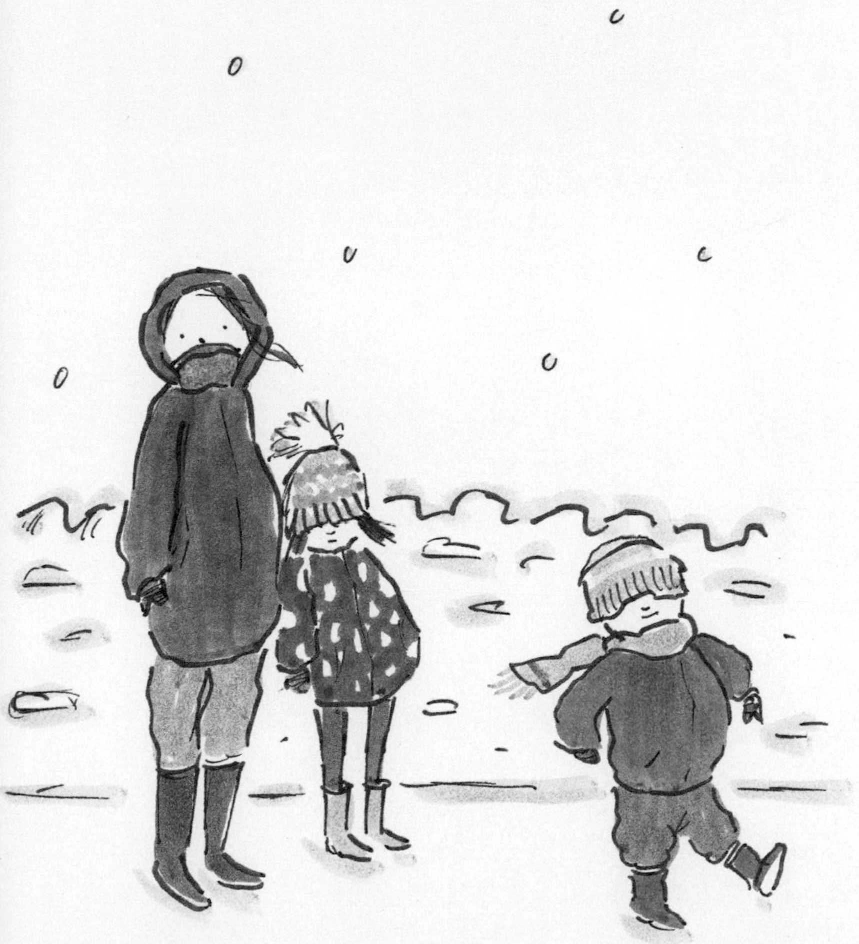

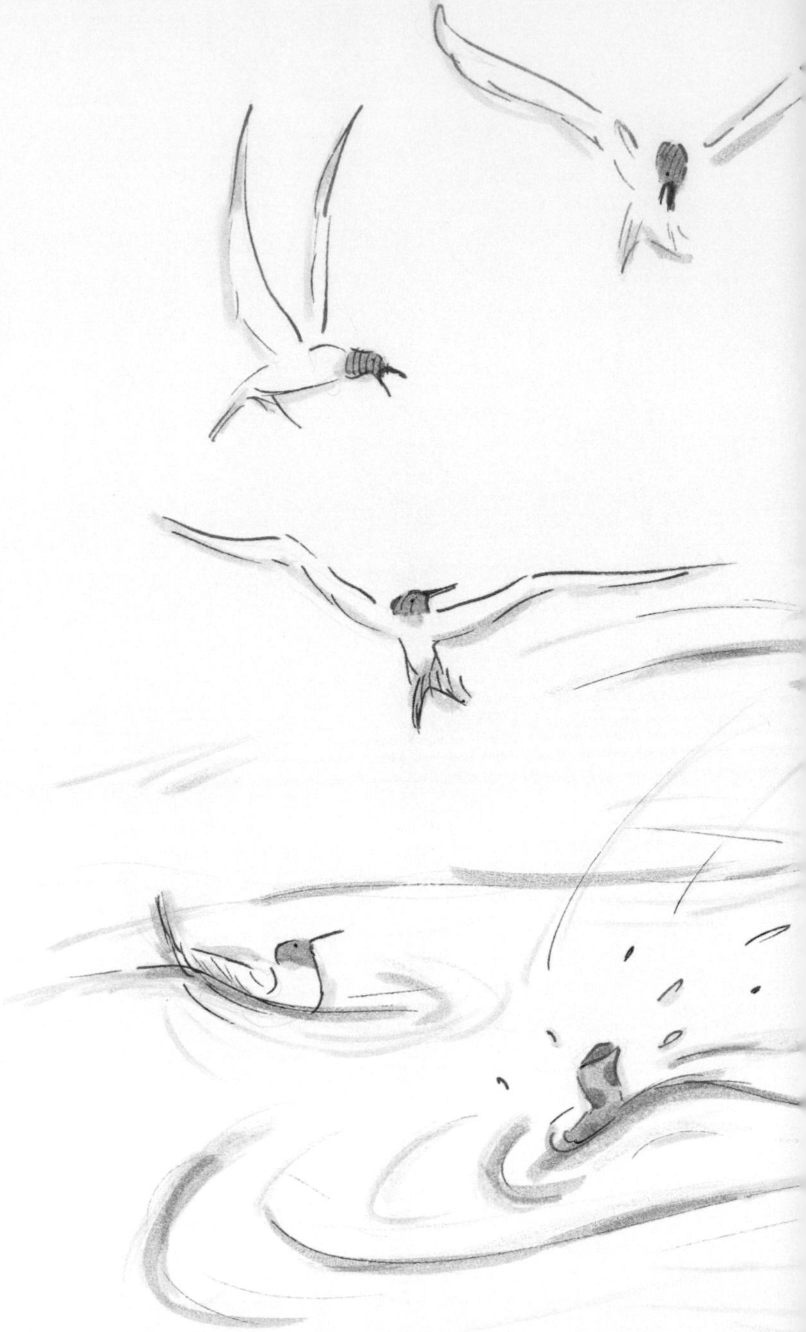

Cinderella never had this problem with wellies...

a rare moment of sitting down

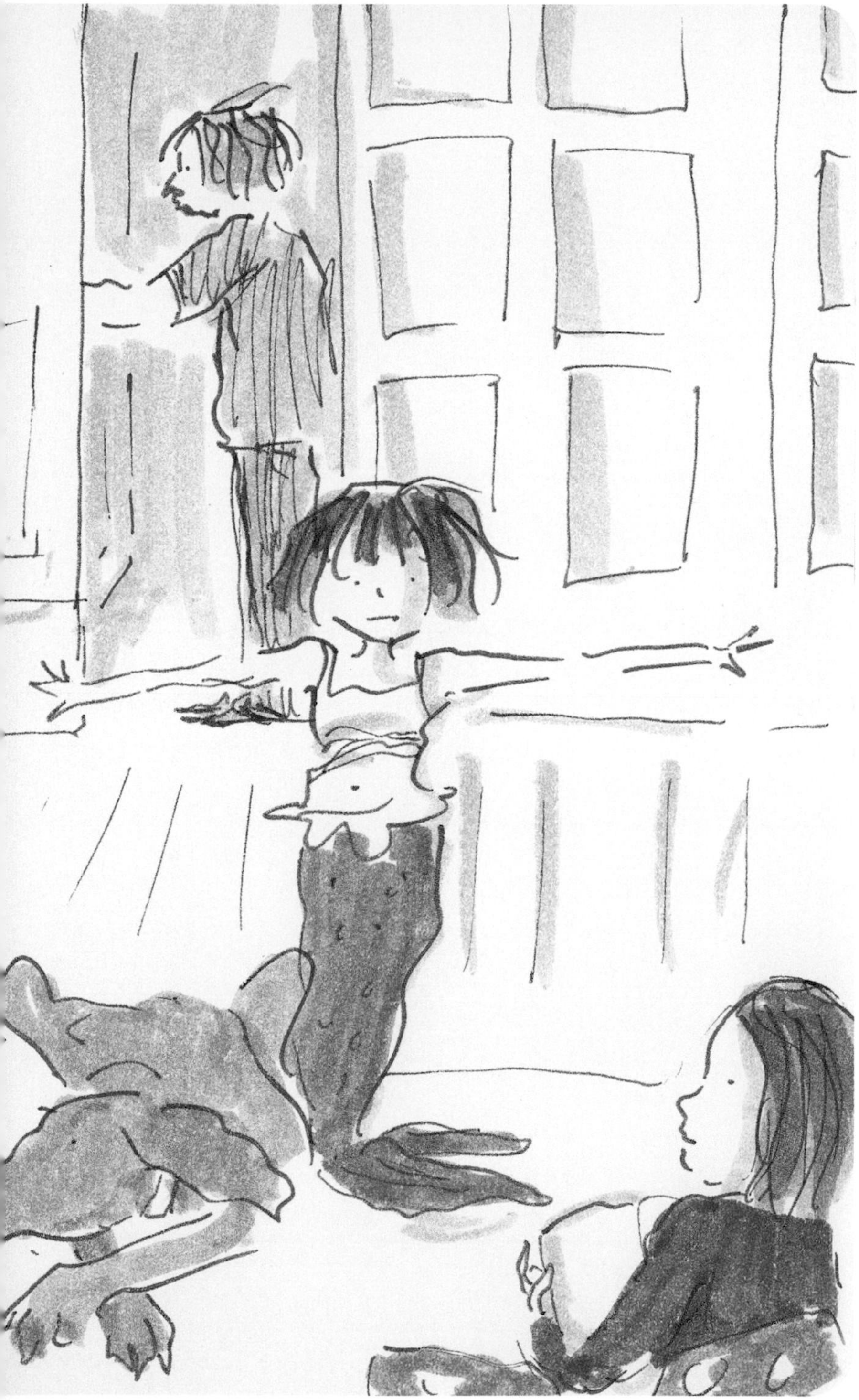

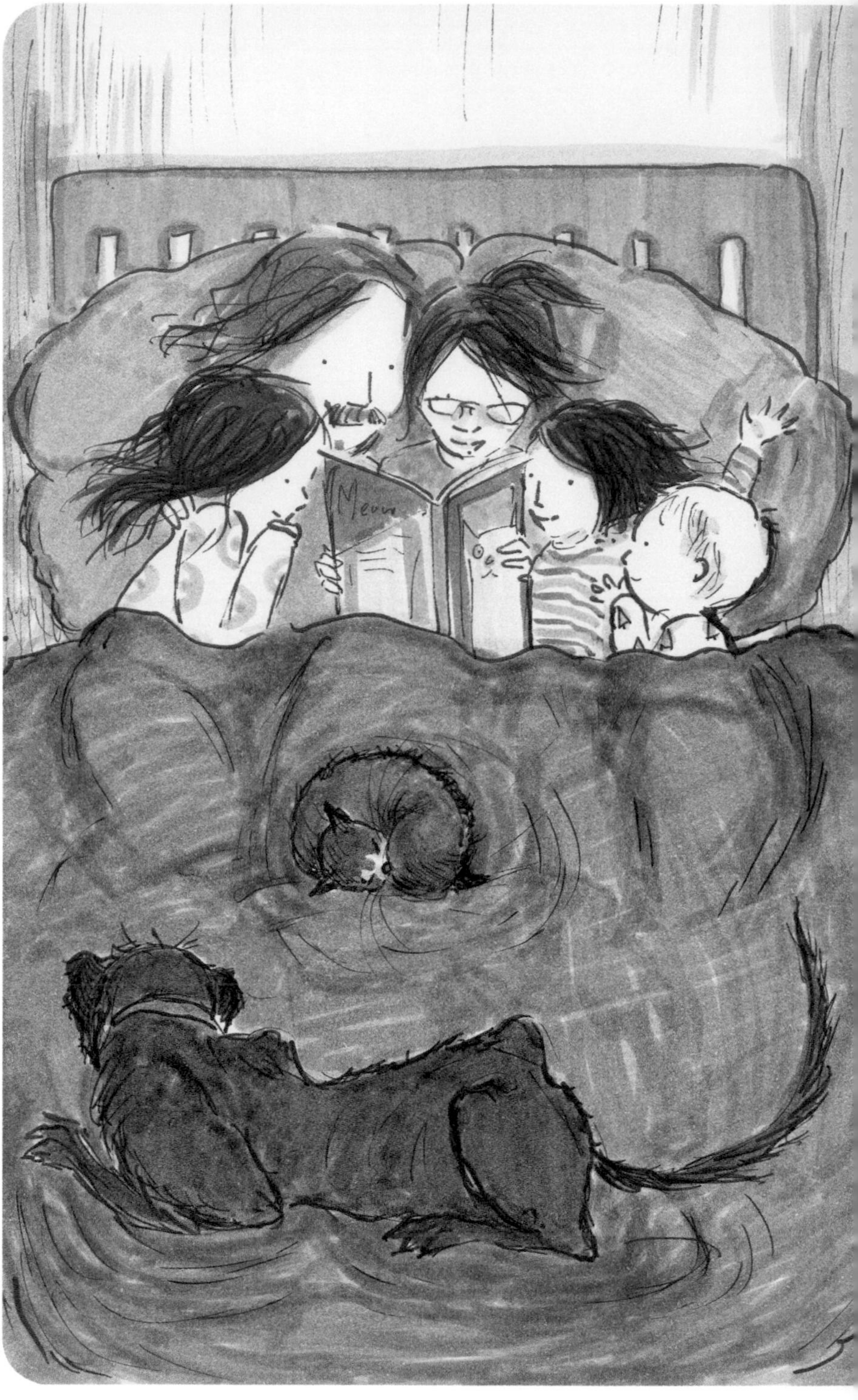
Meow

go to sleep with a story!

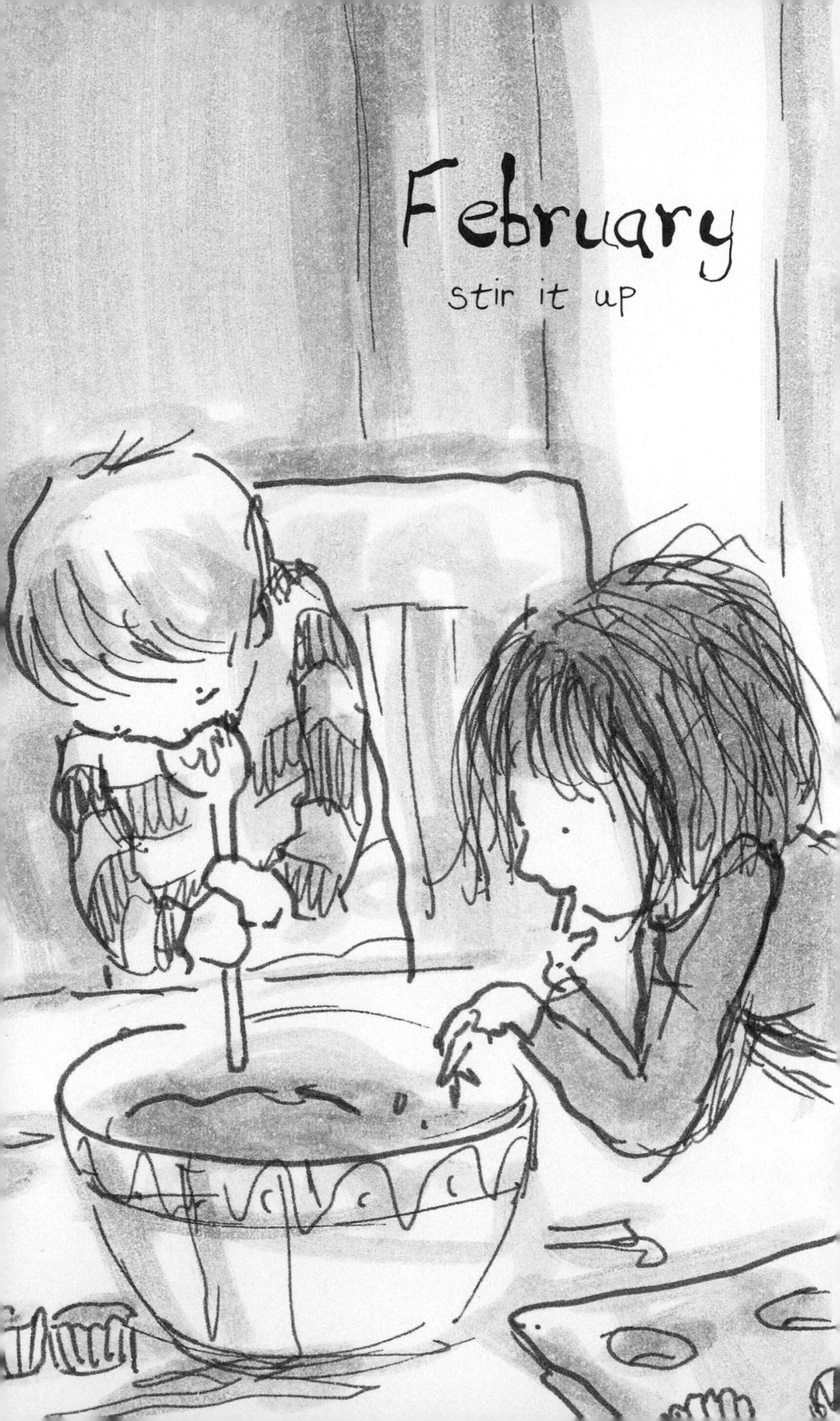
February
stir it up

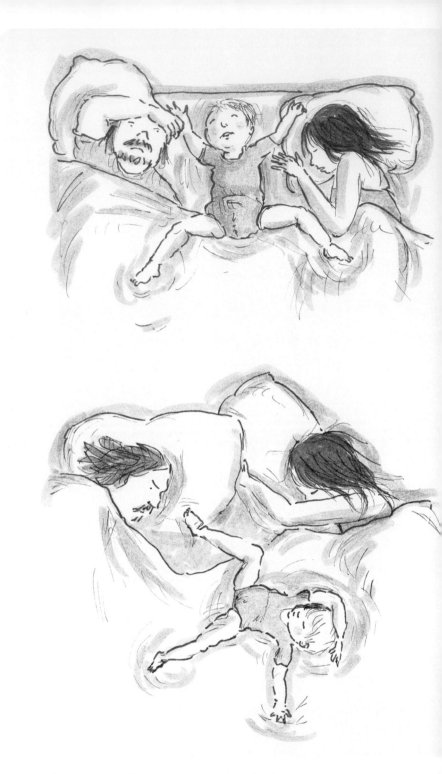

there were three in the bed and the little one said...

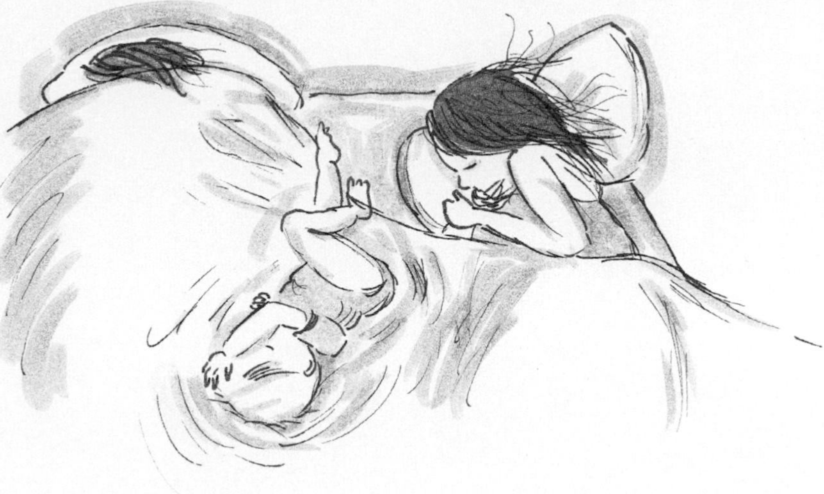

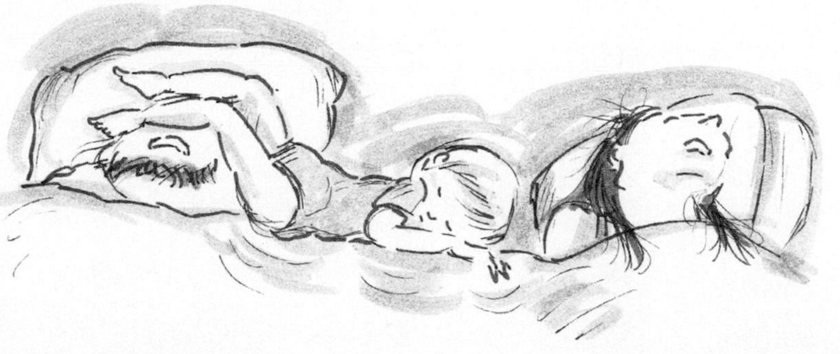

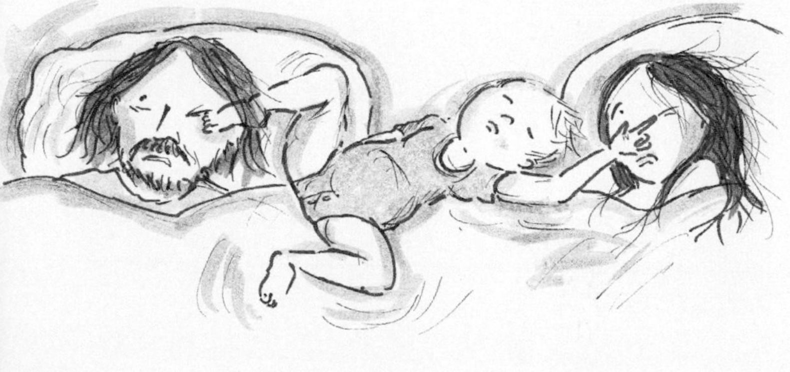

the restaurant will take your orders now...

savouring every mouthful....

...and so appreciative too!

Jam tarts are like a little sea of jam in a world of pastry...

Pancake Day - flippin' marvellous!

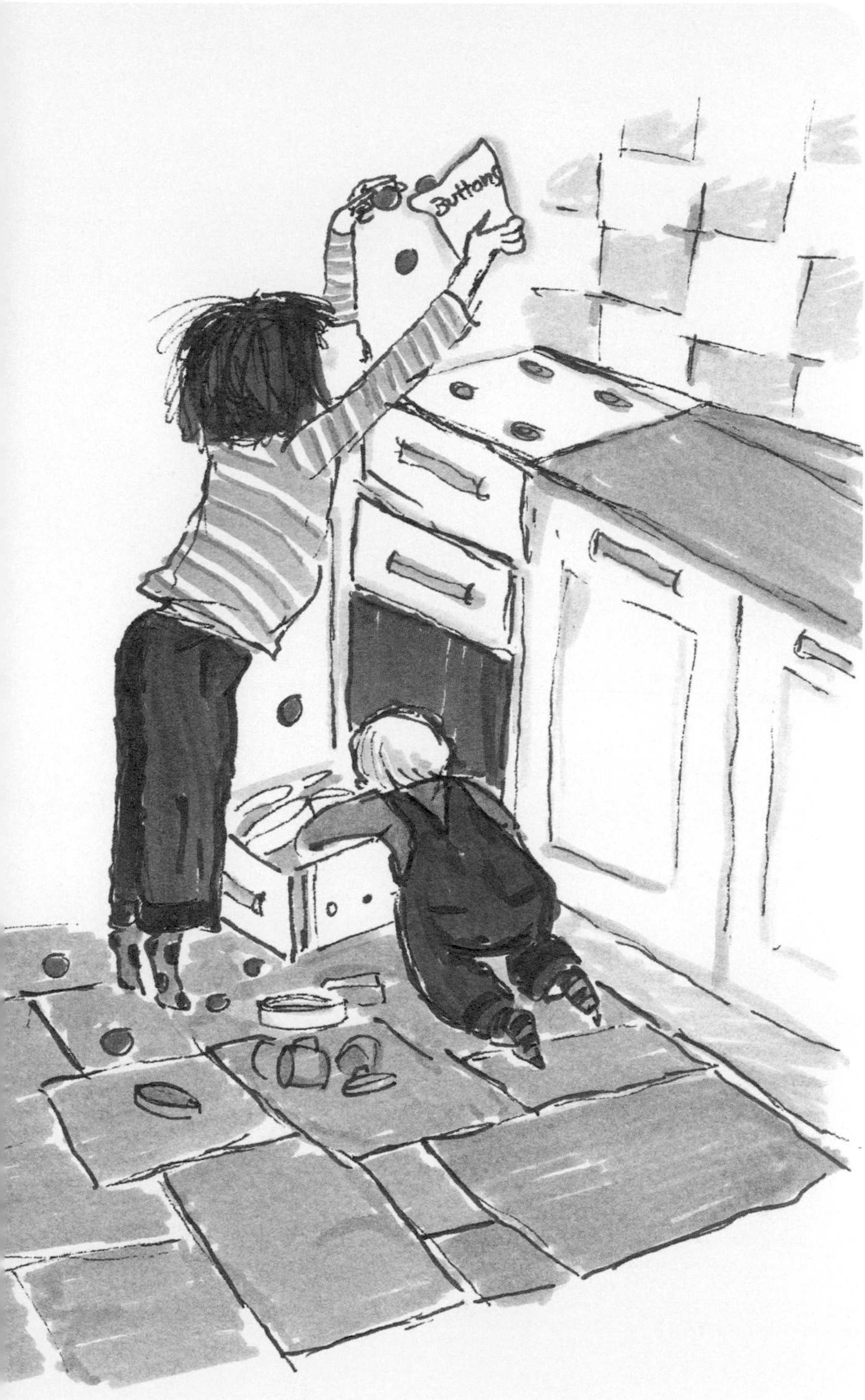
Buttons

kitchen raiders

Mixing...

tasting...

washing up...

Run!

Finished!

will any of the cake mixture make it to the oven?

You bad cake you,
sitting in the KITCHEN
looking at me
all DAY LONG
Teasing my
children.

HOW DARE YOU!

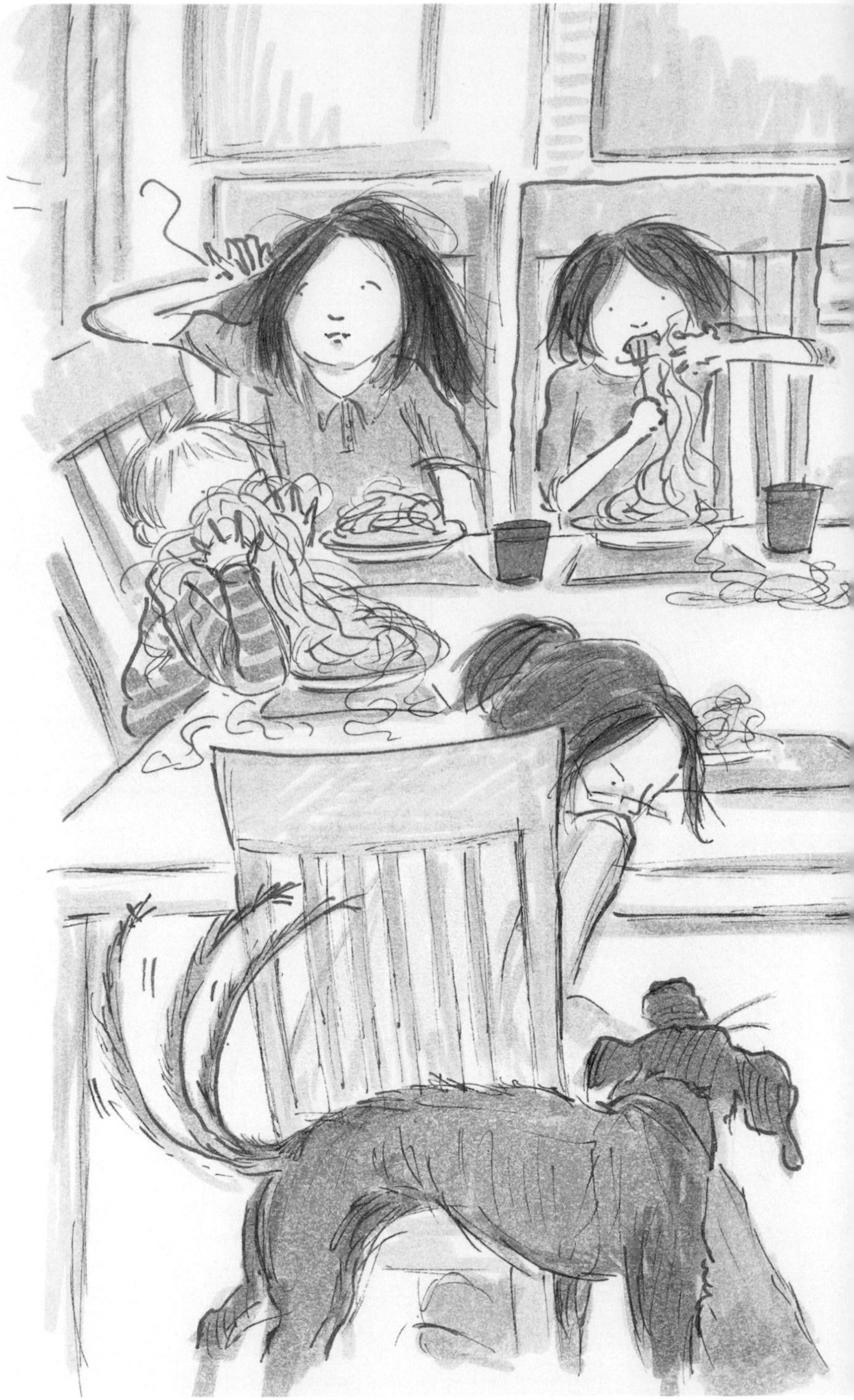

feeding time at the zoo

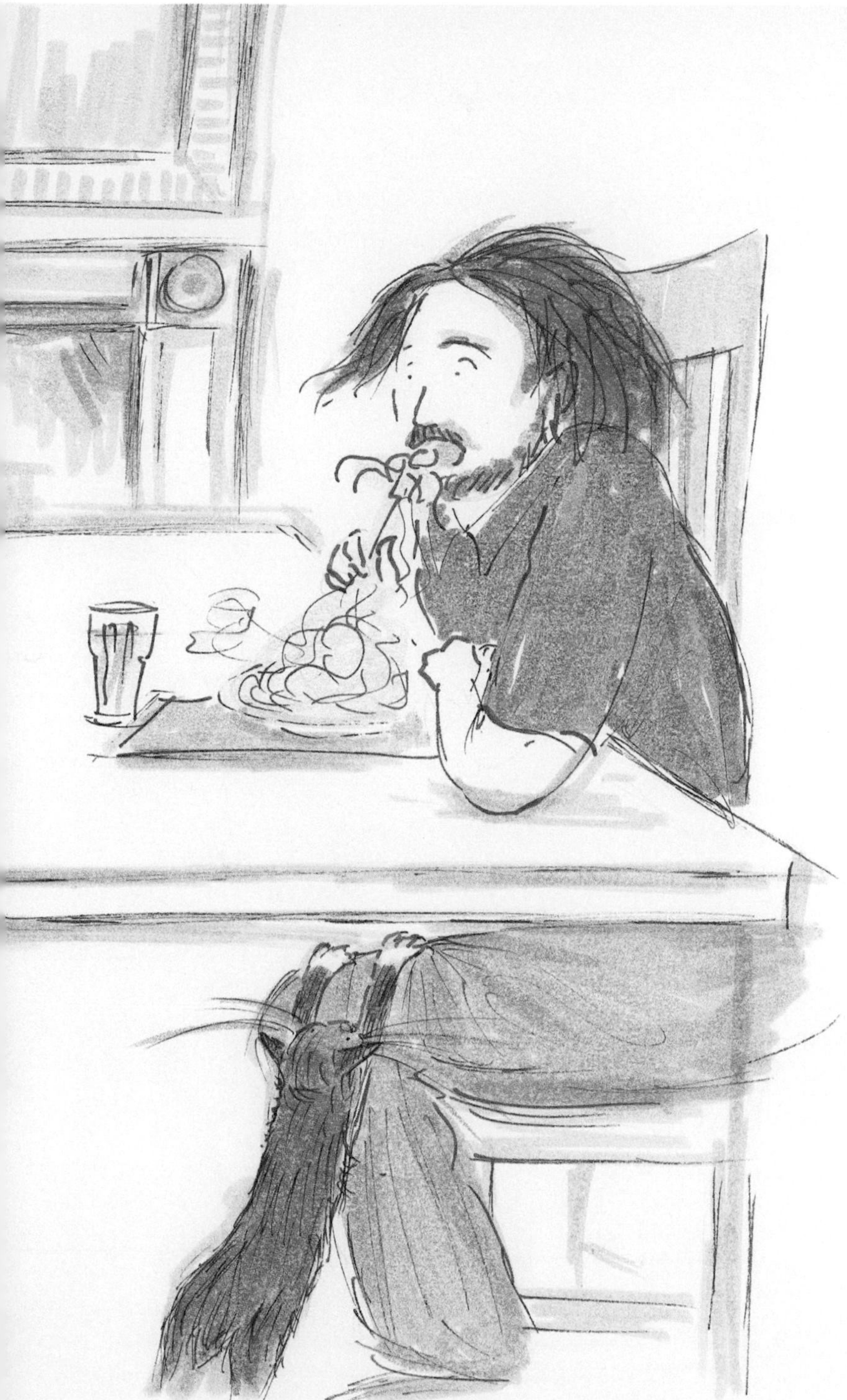

dishwasher Tetris, all the rage you know

March

daffodils, chickens &
'smile for the camera'...

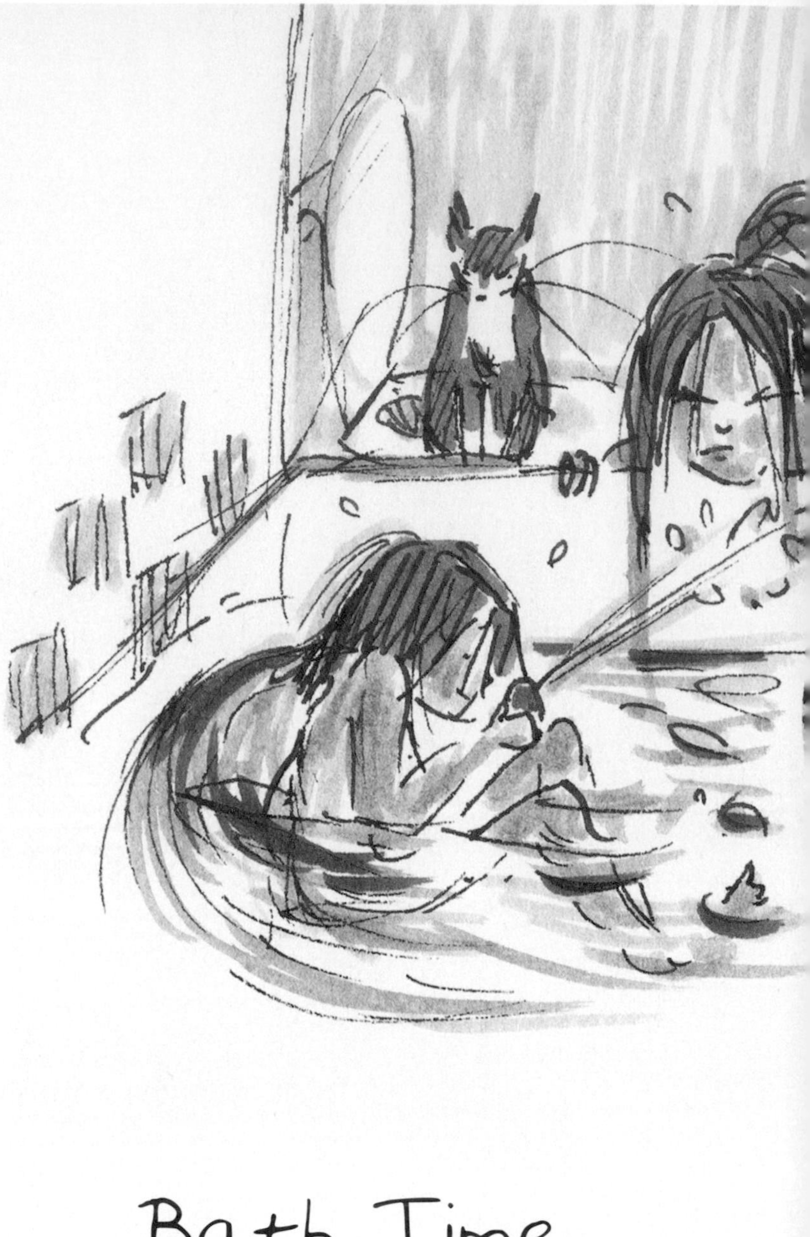

Bath Time

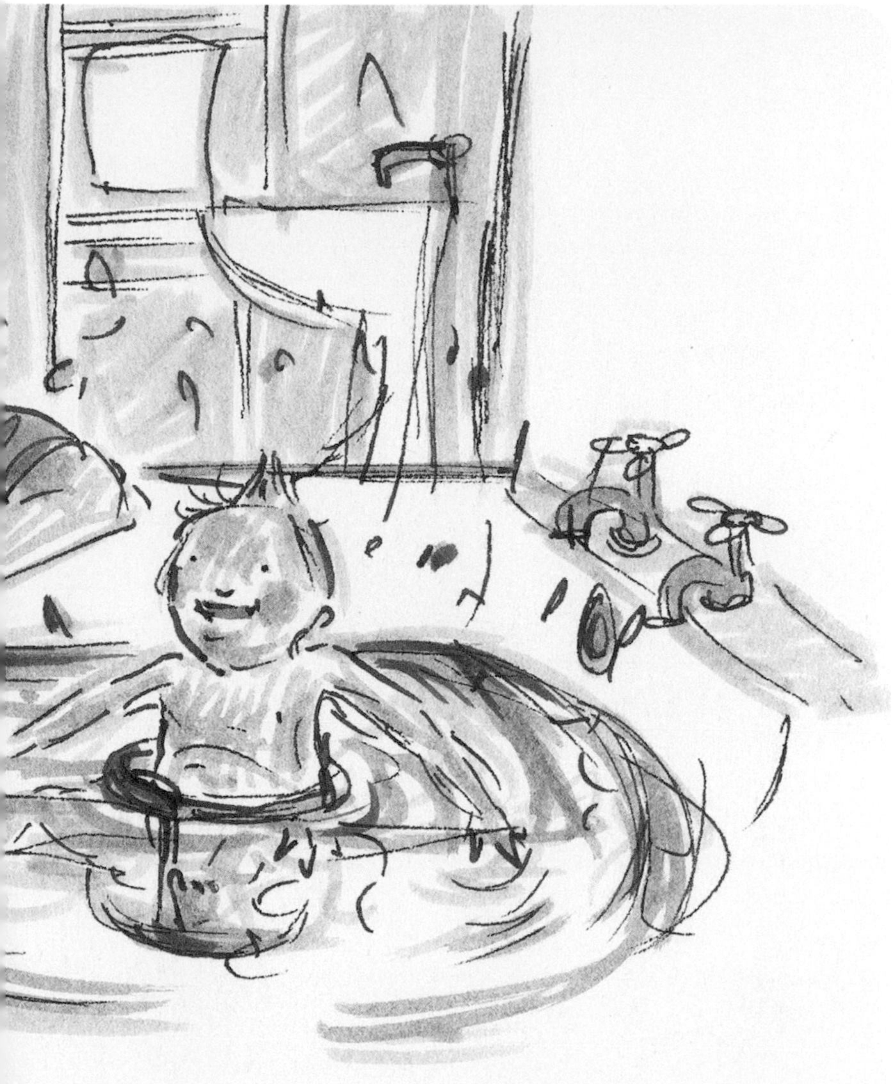

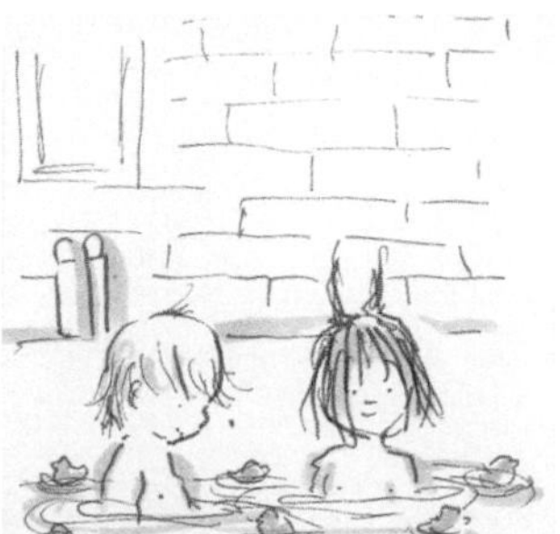

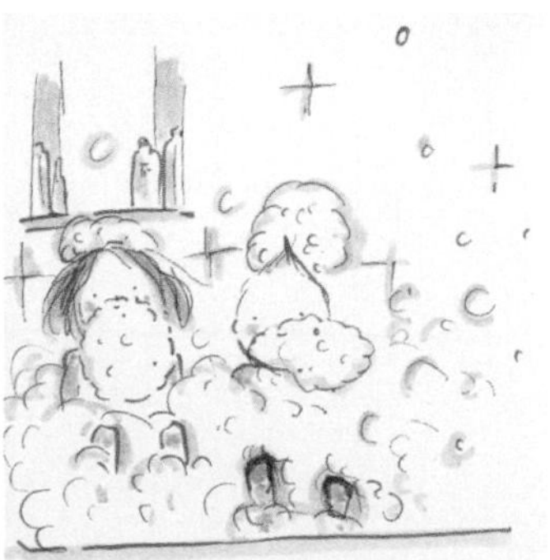

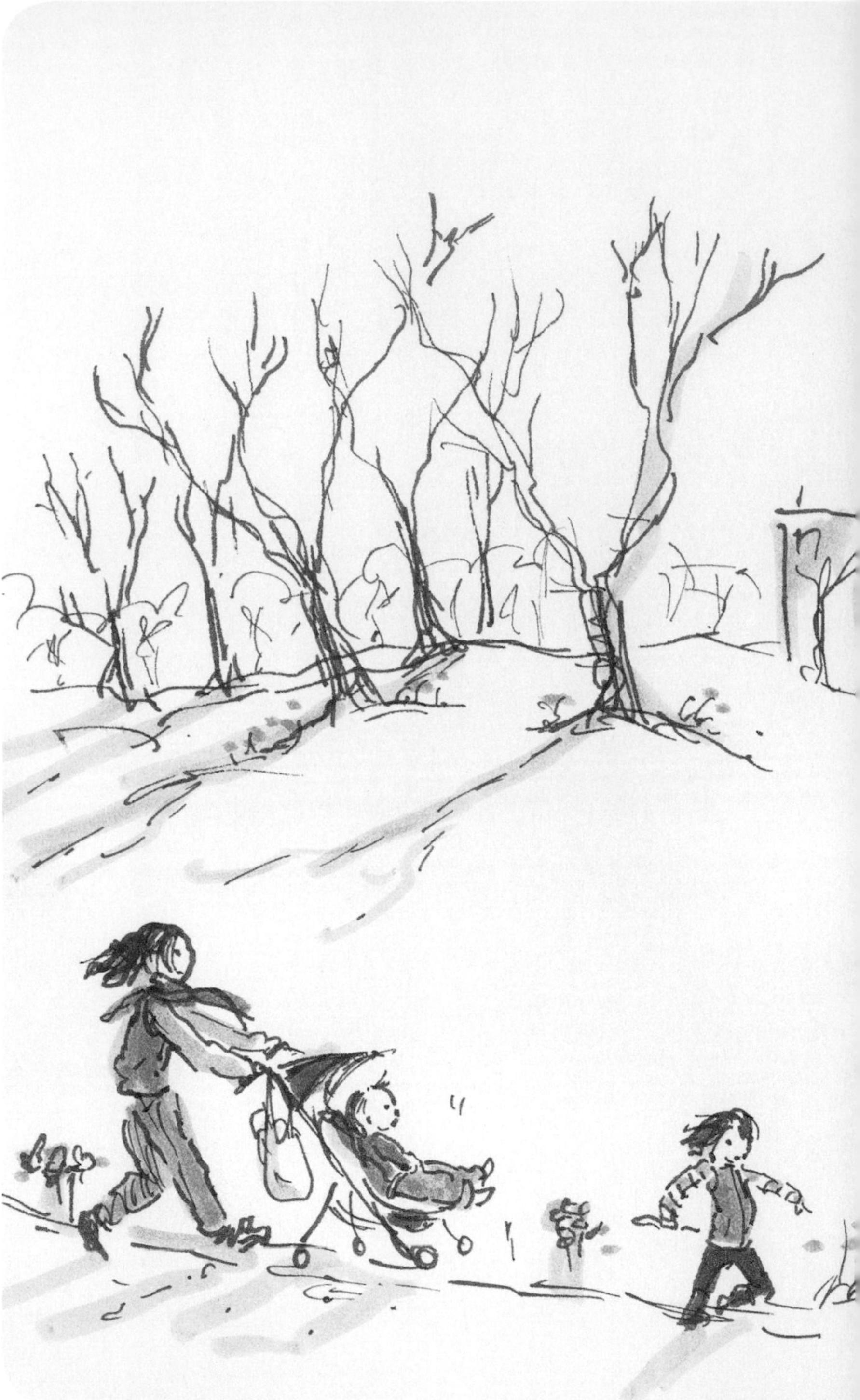

a walk in Echo Park

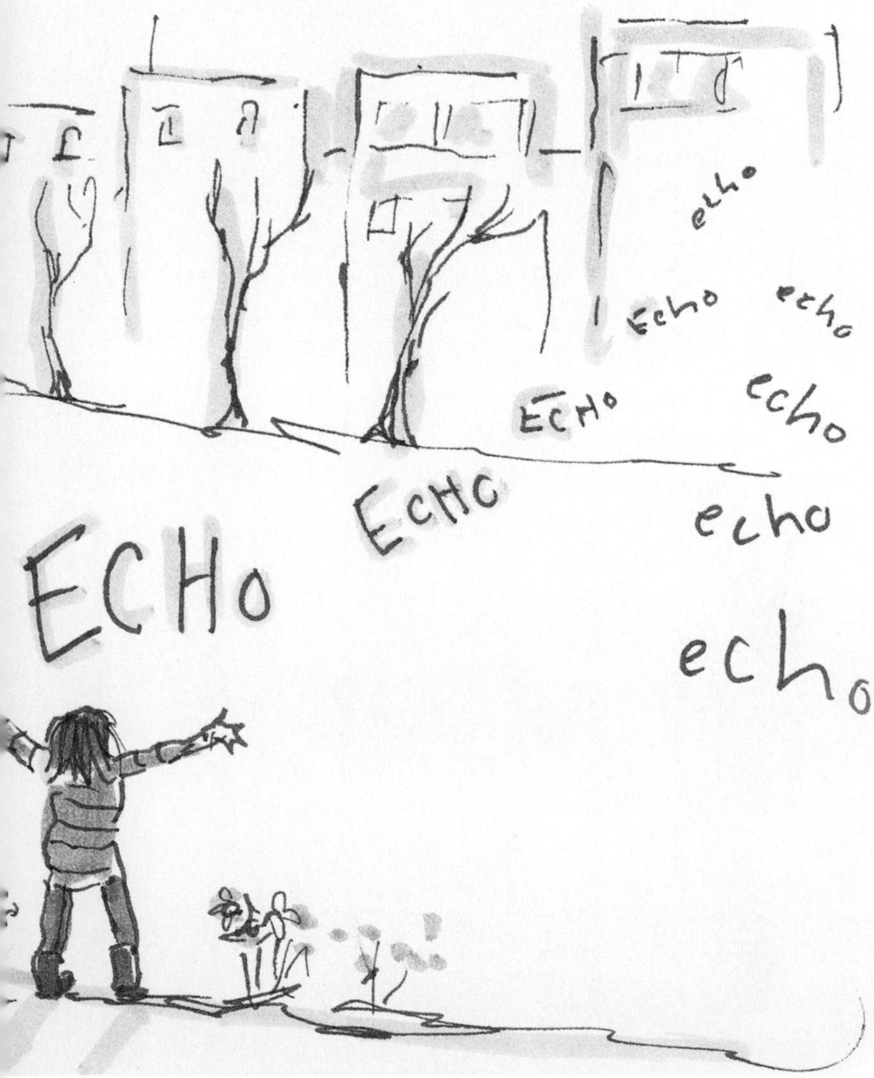
echo
Echo
echo
ECHO
echo
ECHO
echo
ECHO
echo

St David's Day, national costumes on and daffodils at the ready!

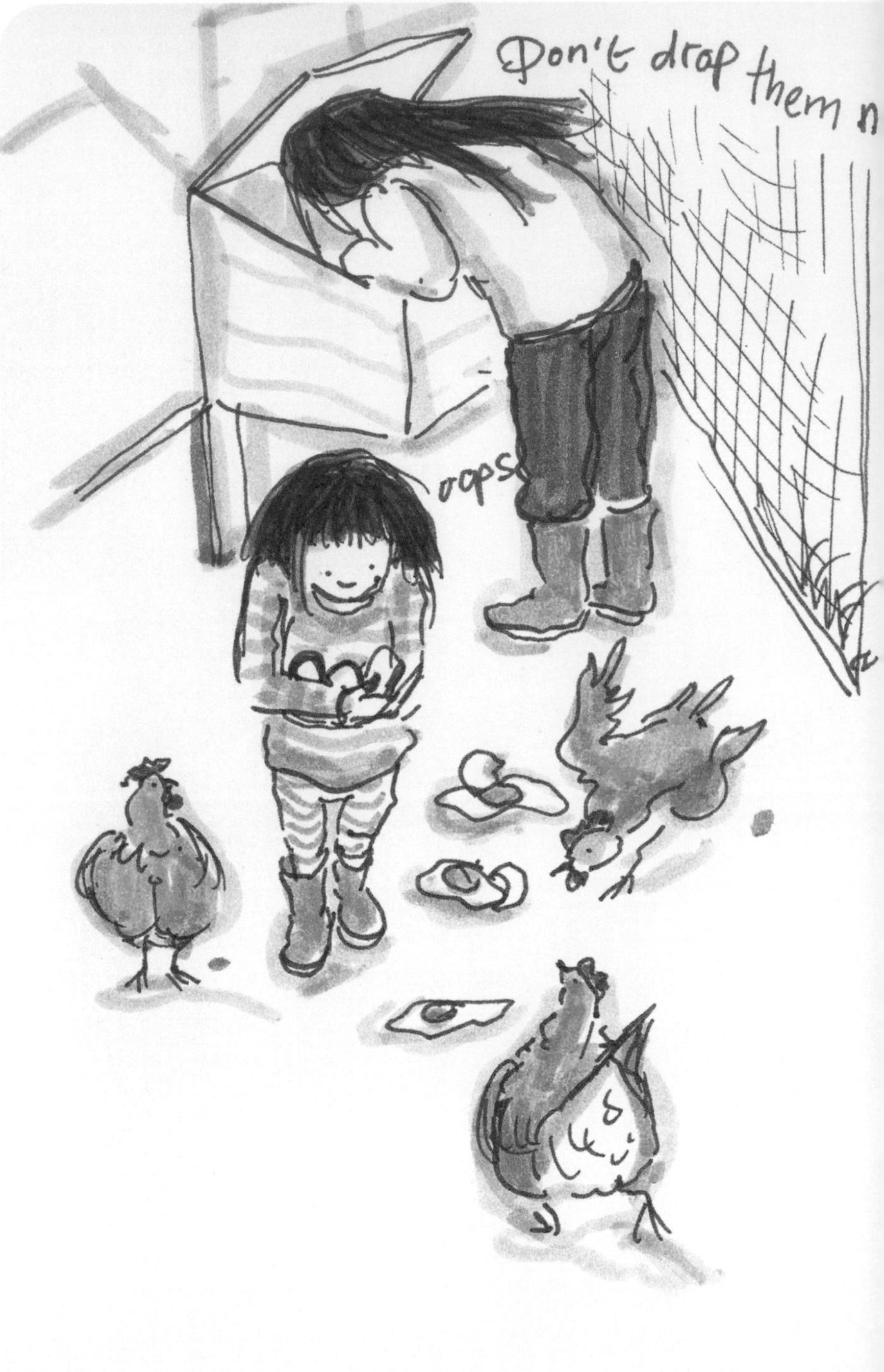
Don't drop them n
oops

egg collectors

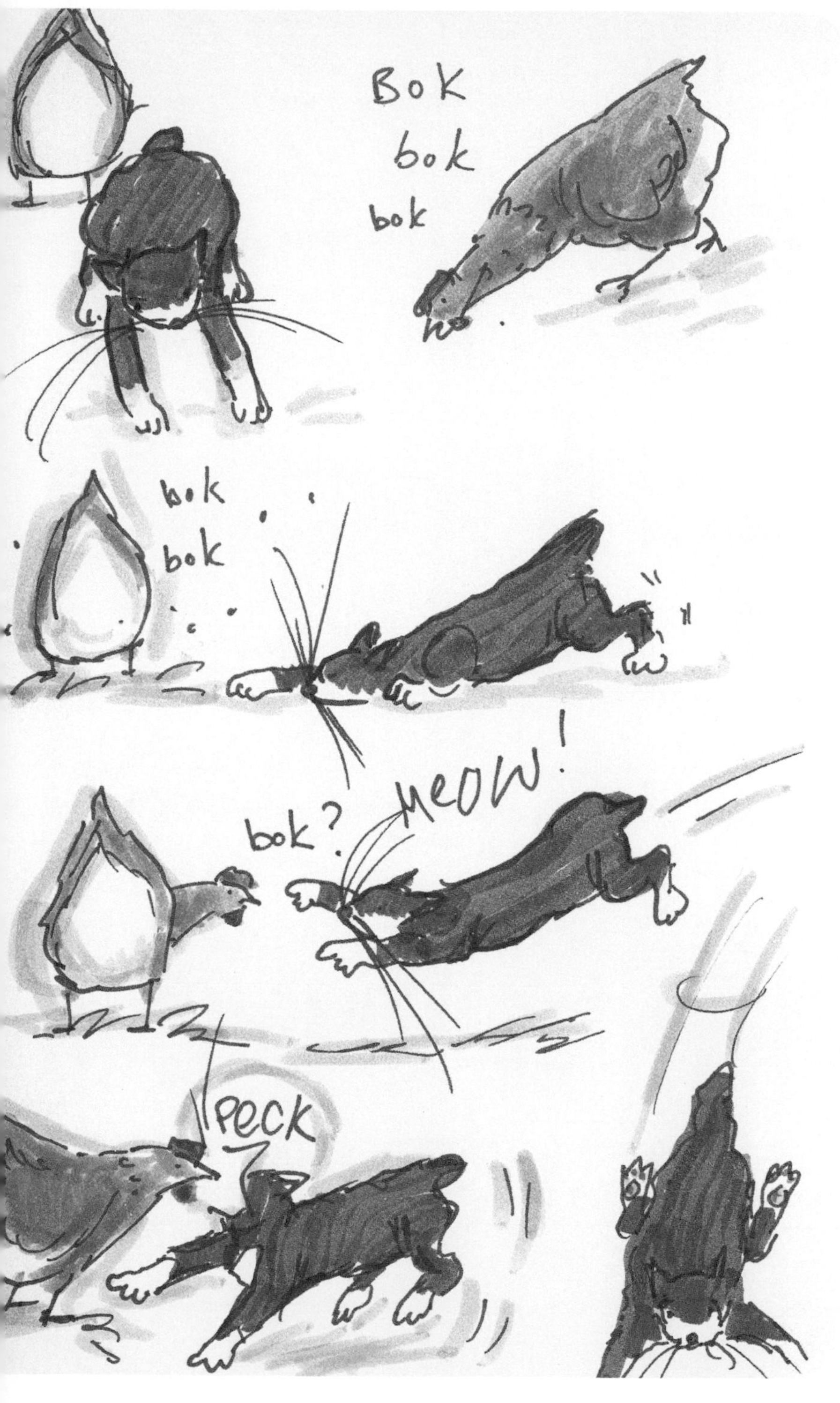
Bok
bok
bok
bok
bok
bok?
MeOW!
Peck

egg defenders!

wiggly worms and hungry hens

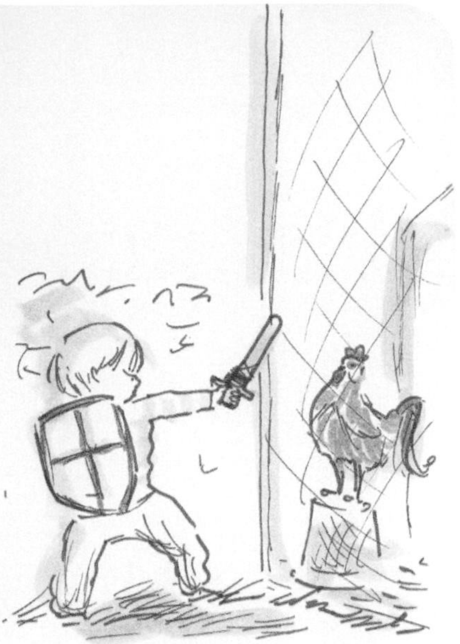

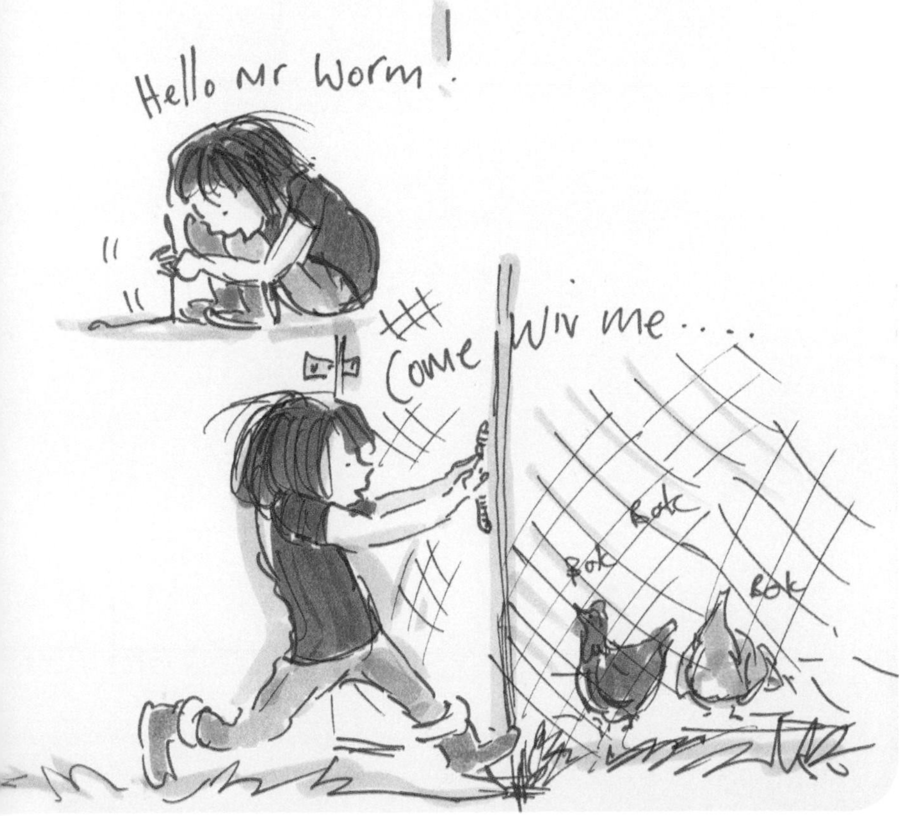
Hello mr Worm!
Come wiv me . . . .
Bok
Bok
Bok

Mother's Day

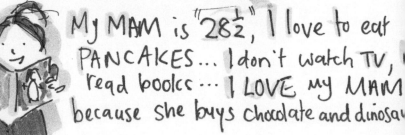

My MAM is "28½", I love to eat PANCAKES... I don't watch TV, I read books... I LOVE MY MAM because she buys chocolate and dinosa

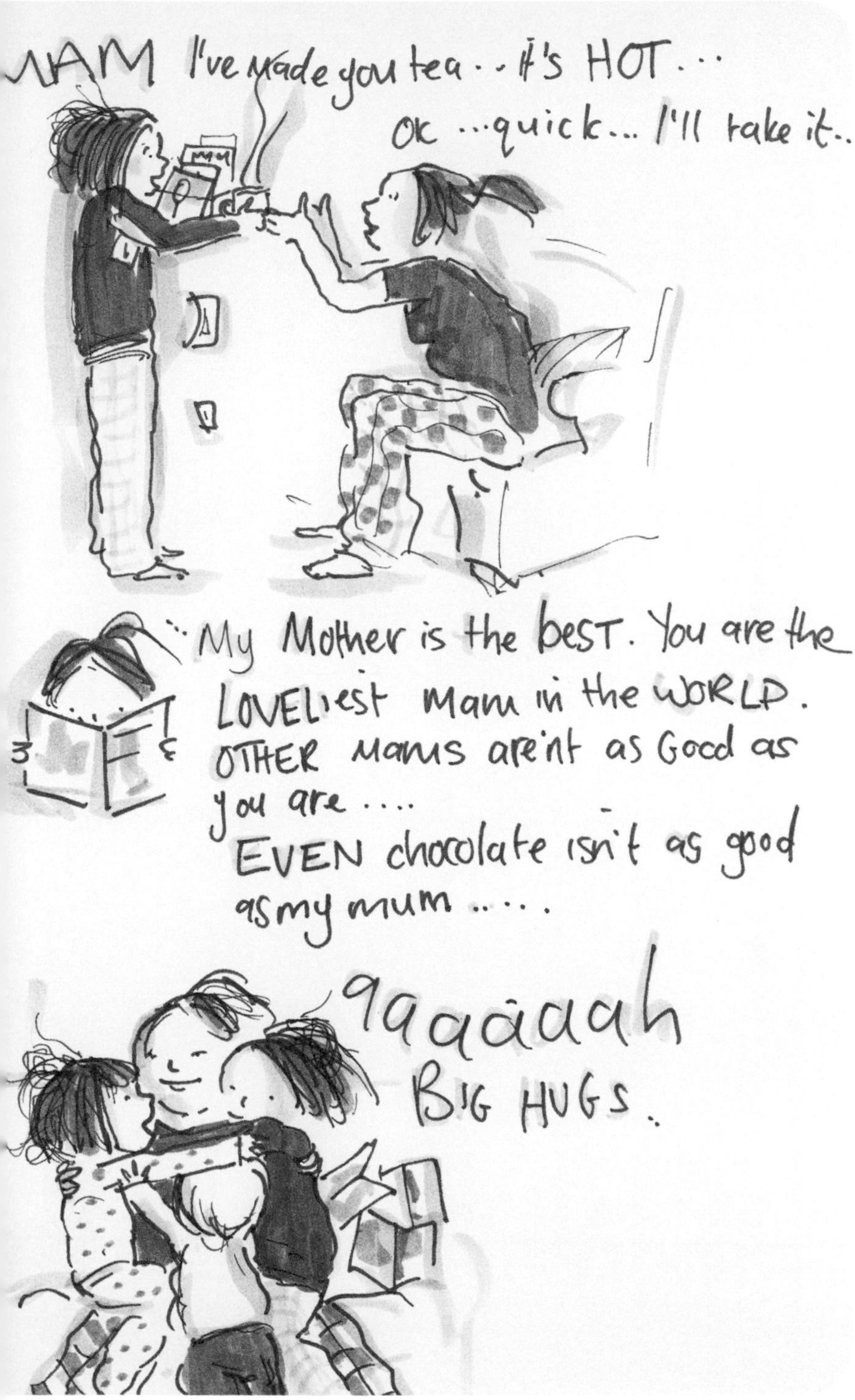
MAM I've made you tea.. it's HOT...
OK ...quick... I'll take it..
...My Mother is the BEST. You are the LOVELiest Mam in the WORLD. OTHER Mams are'nt as Good as you are....
EVEN chocolate isn't as good as my mum.....
aaaaaah
BIG HUGS..

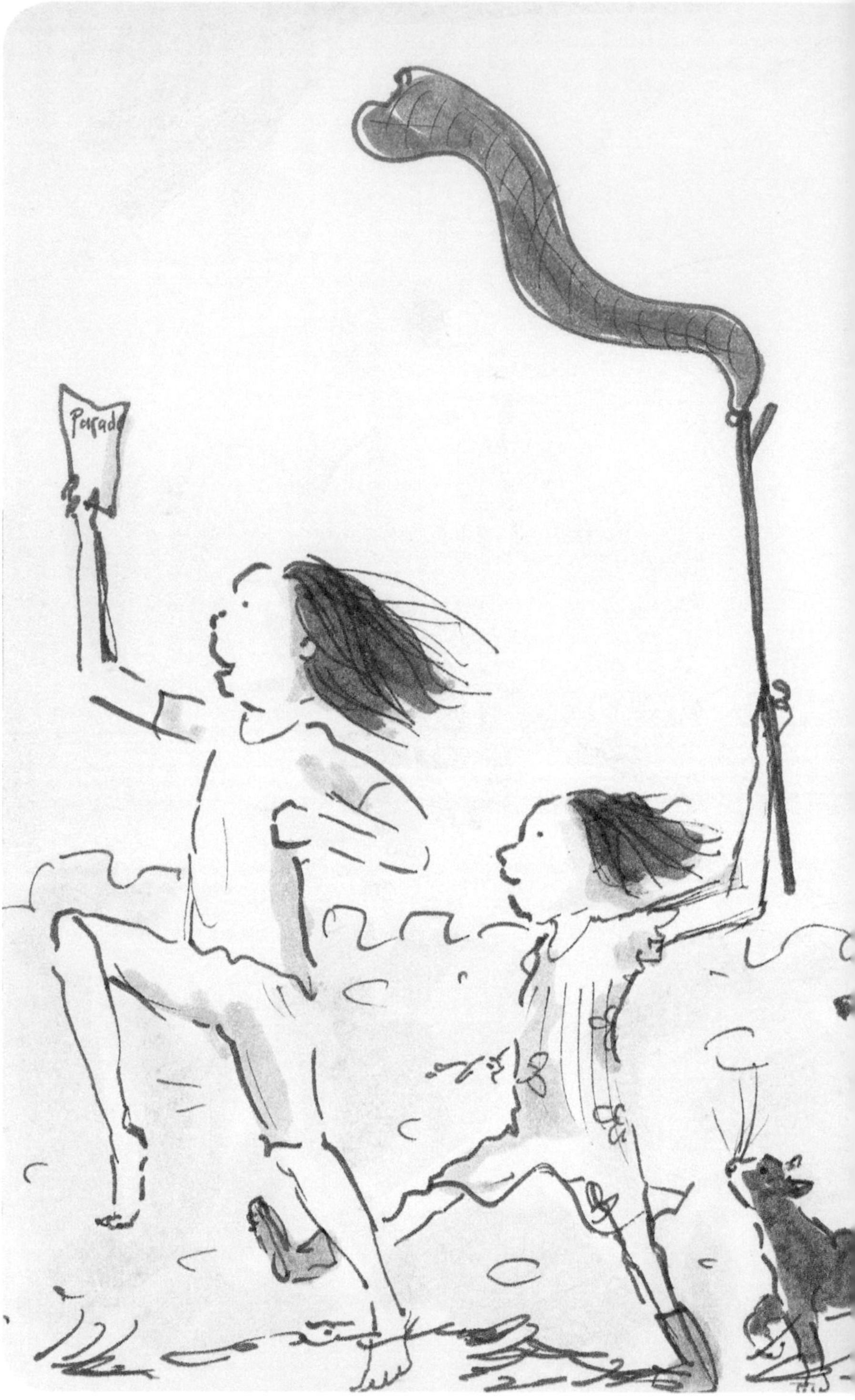
Parade

let's have a parade!

sometimes I feel very lucky to be a mum

April

spring has sprung

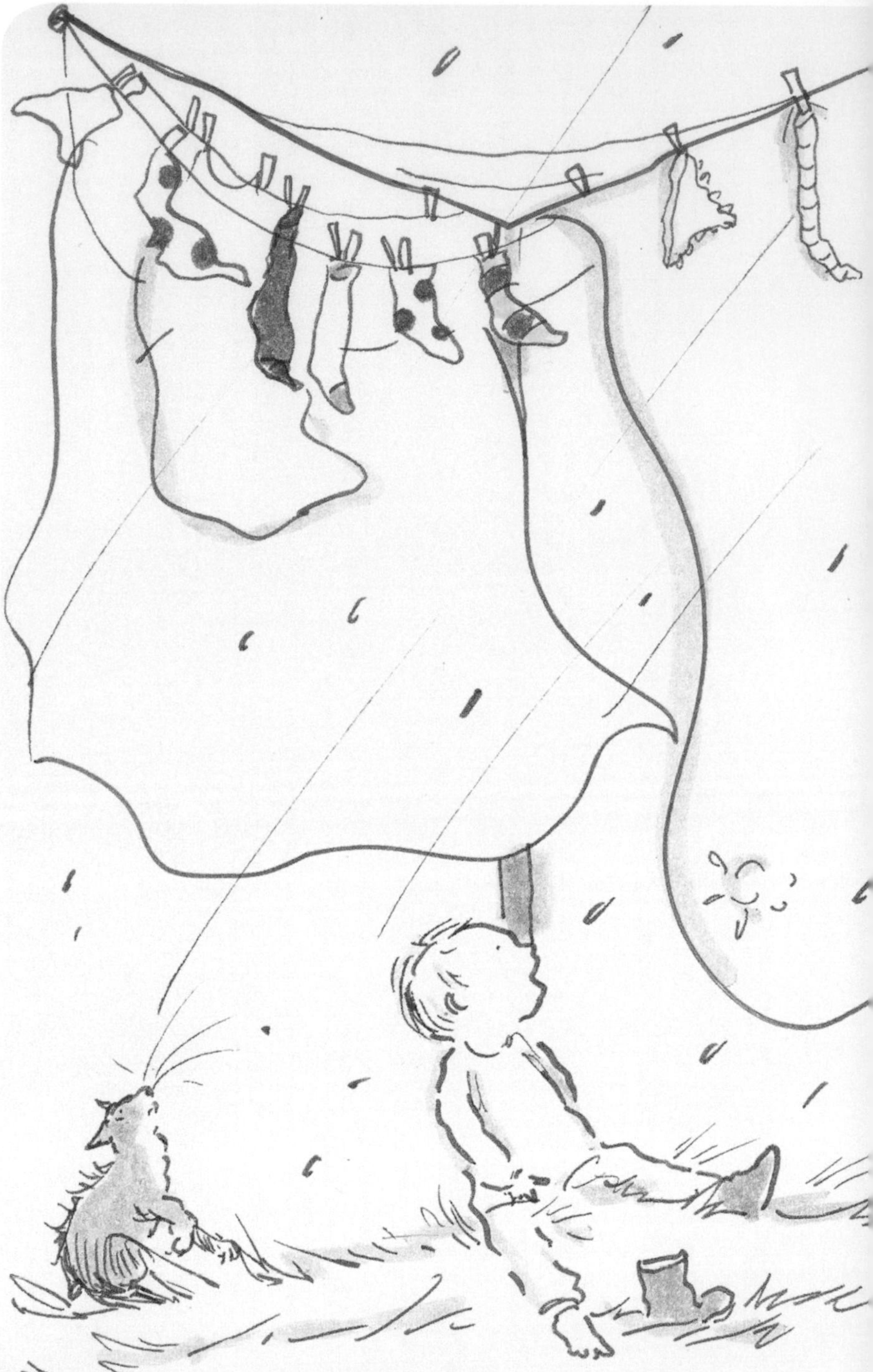

April showers

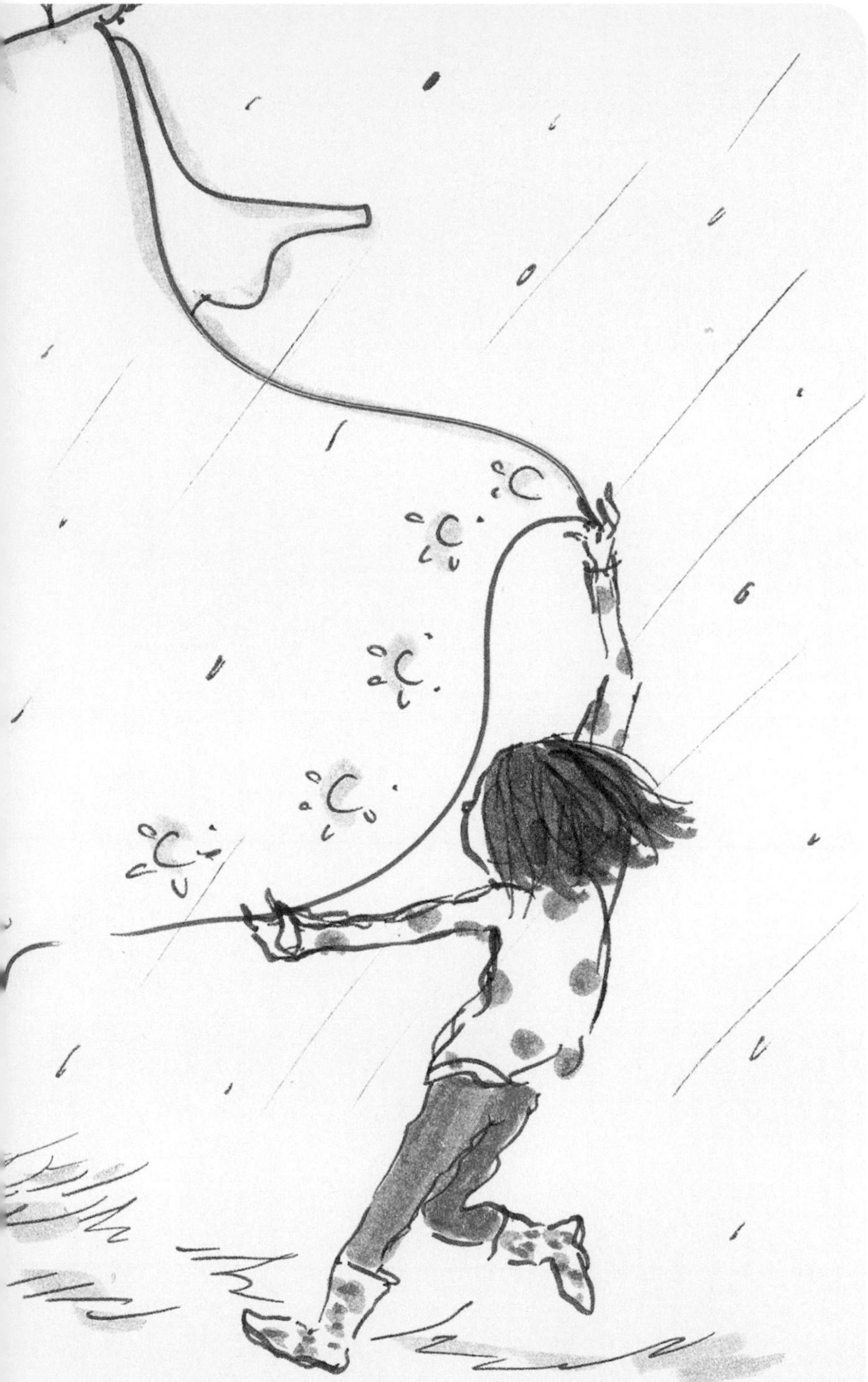

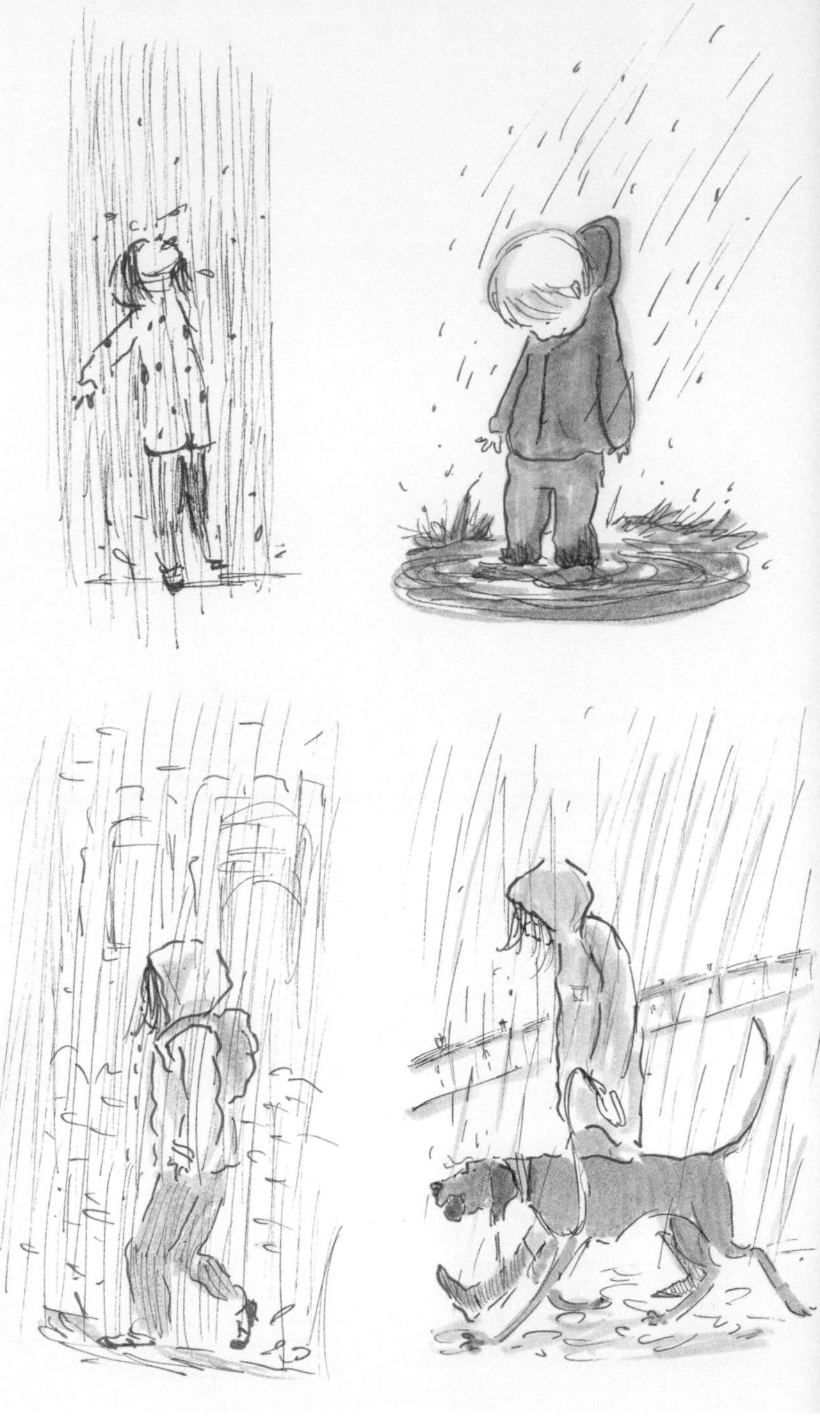

Rain rain go away...

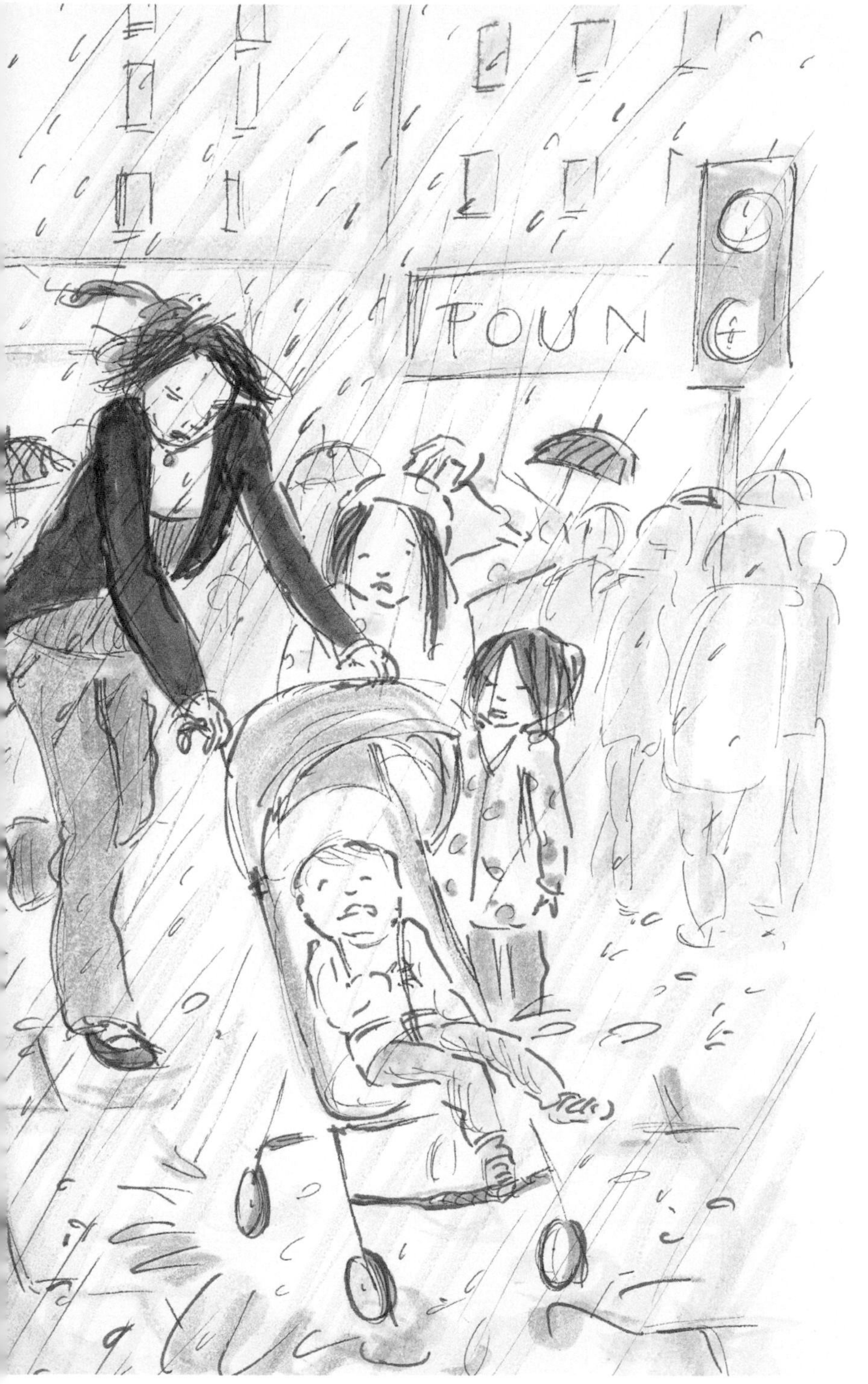
POUN

The Easter Bonnet towering inferno...

I Found an egg!

we're going on an egg hunt!

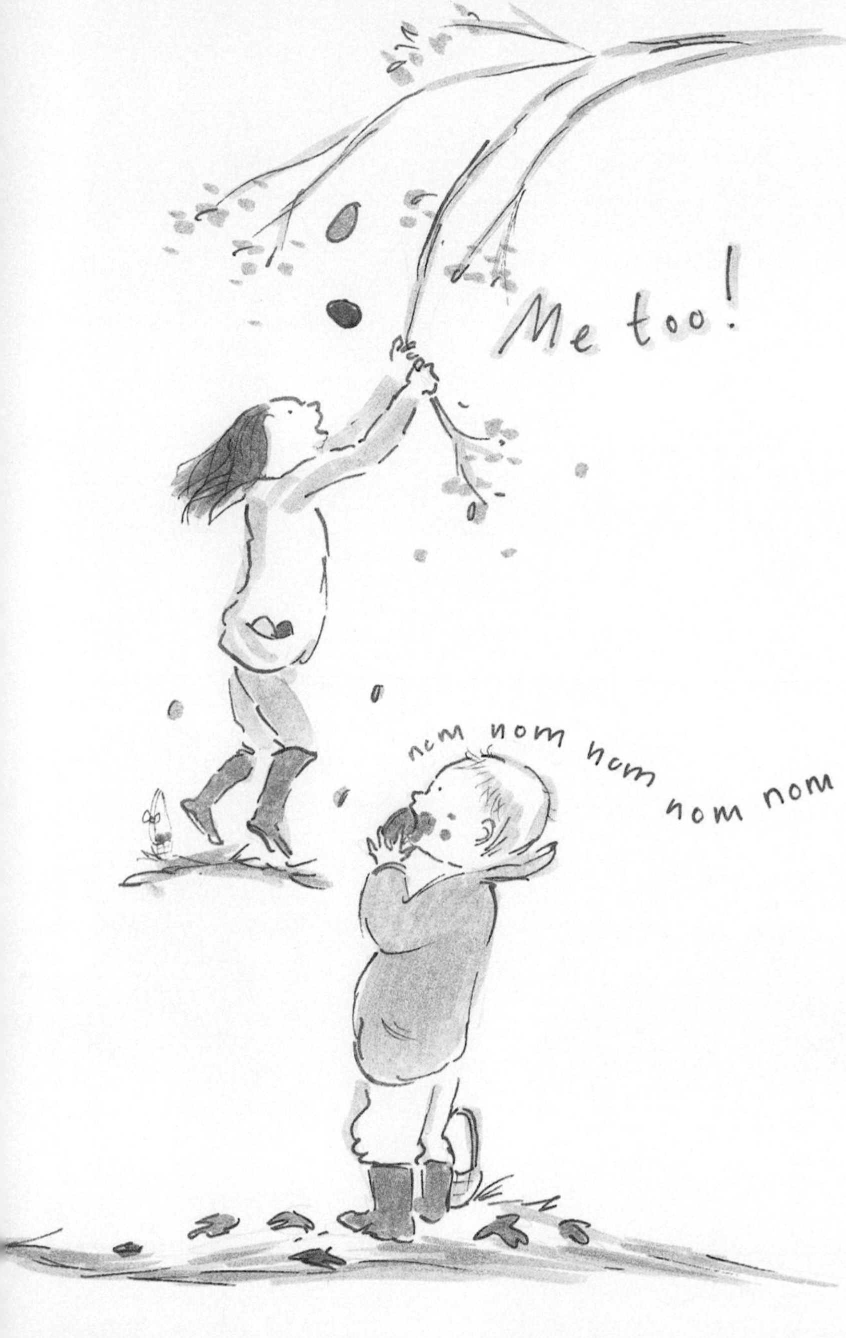
Me too!
nom nom nom nom nom

the effects of too many Easter eggs...

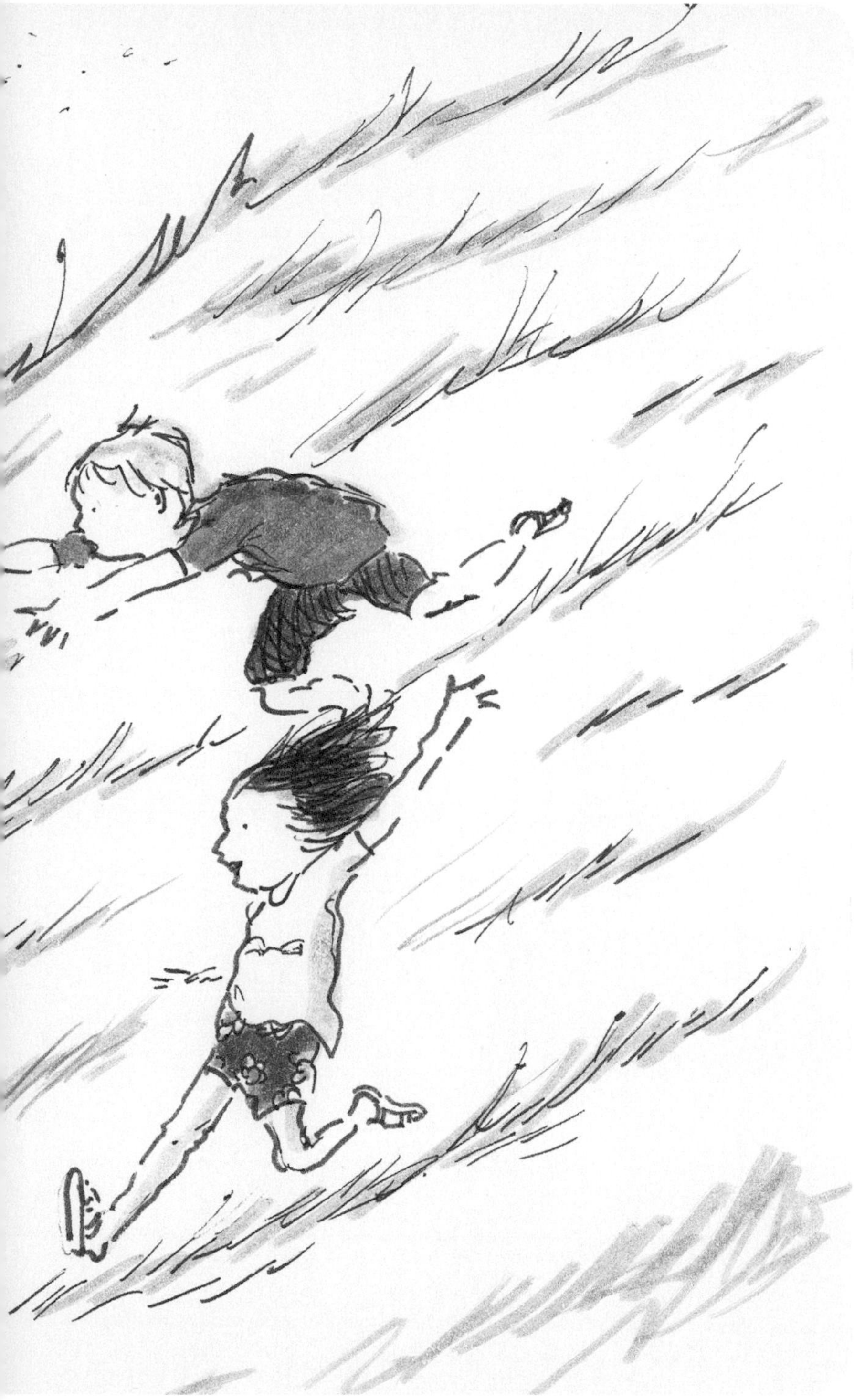

had enough chocolate yet Gruff?

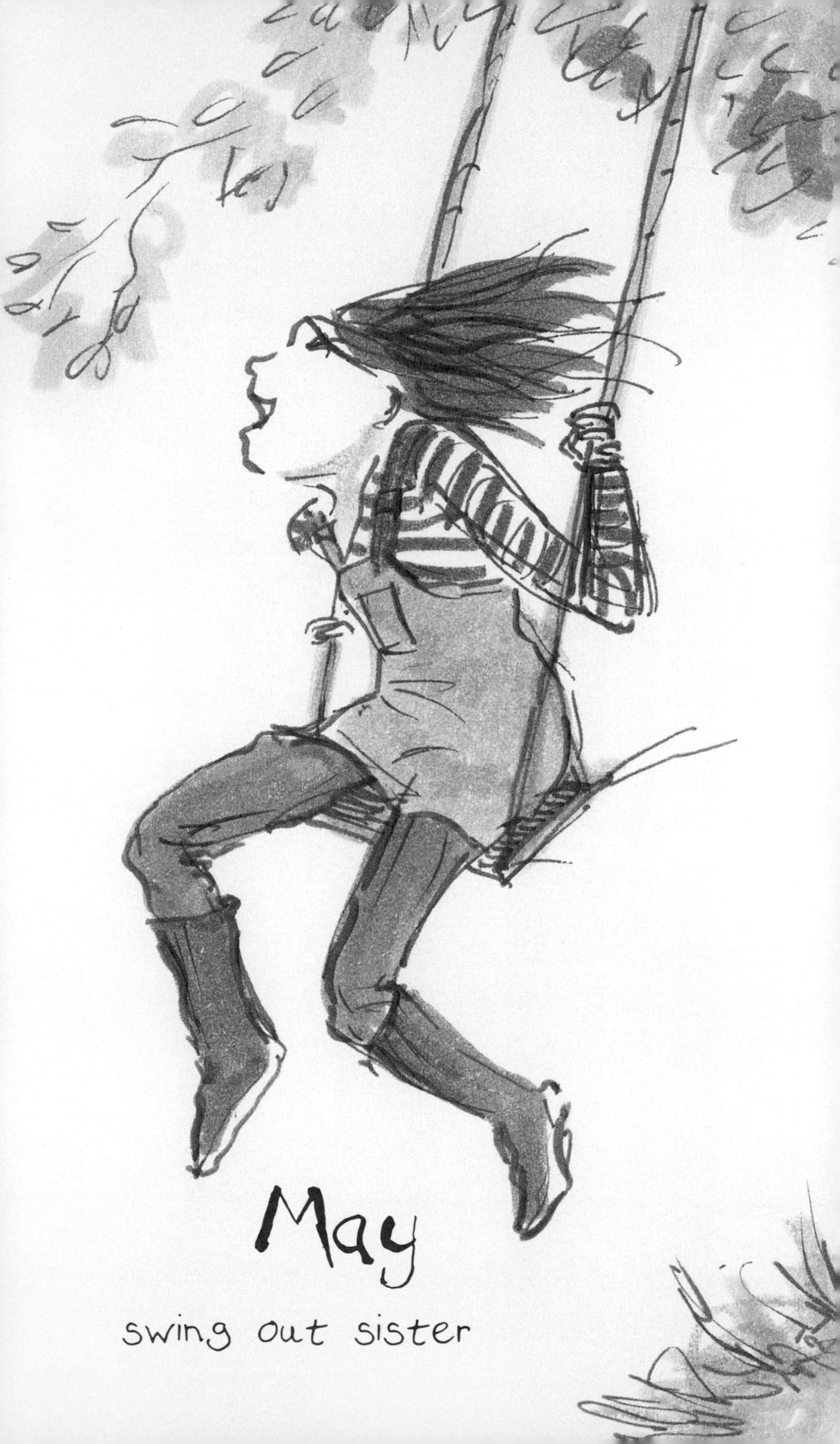

May

swing out sister

Miss Millie Soapbox - keeping it real

not the role models she wants

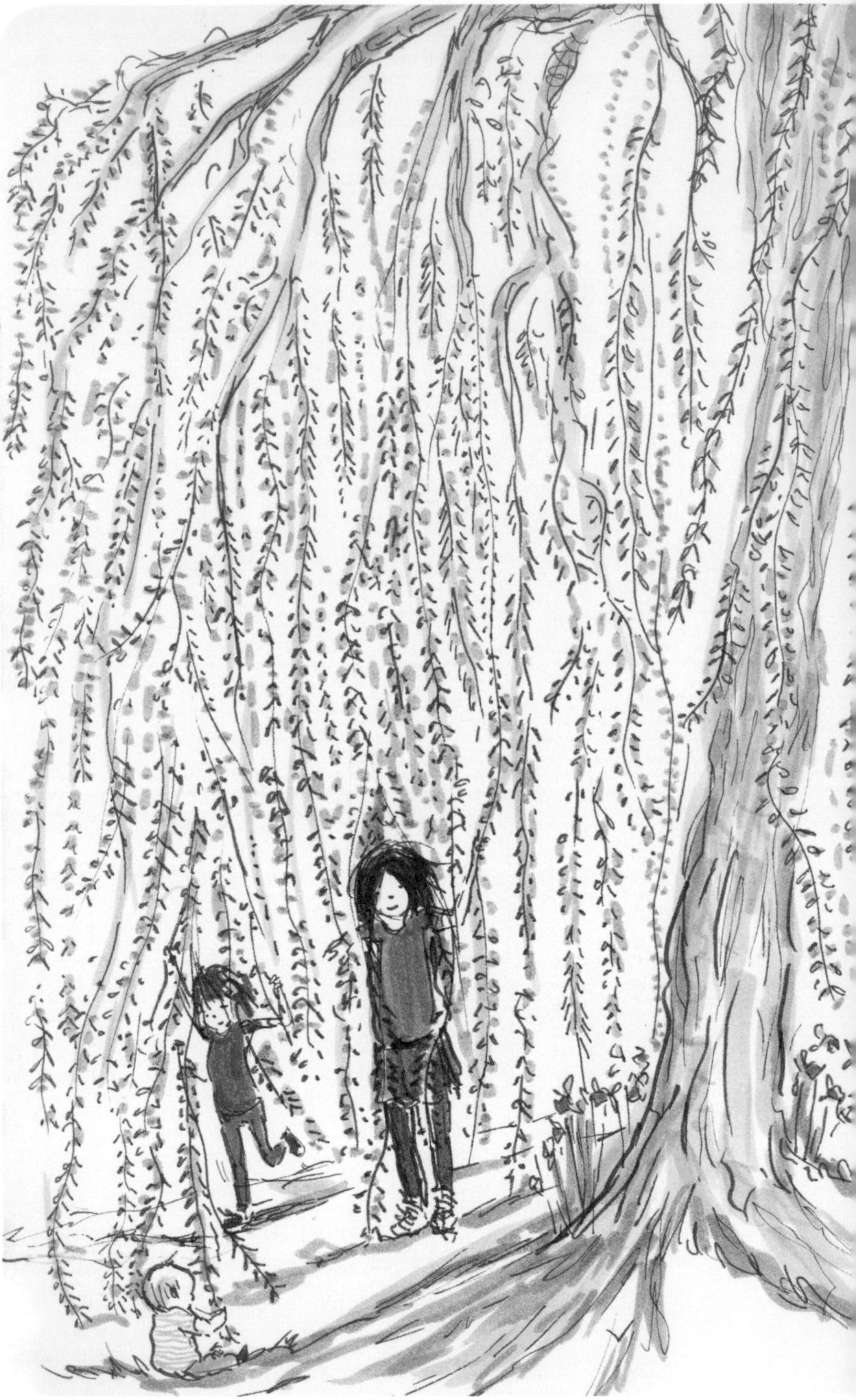

big sisters are lovely

someone to hide behind and look after you...

...and do everything they tell you to do!

big sister made us do it!

a multi-talented big sister

Mam .. we found a jewel at school...
oh right?
Yeah it's brill, I can TALK to it...
I JUST put my fingers here and listen...
So these are my jewels...
COOL!
What are they saying?
I dunno ... they're all talking at once...

never a dull moment when you have a big sister like this!

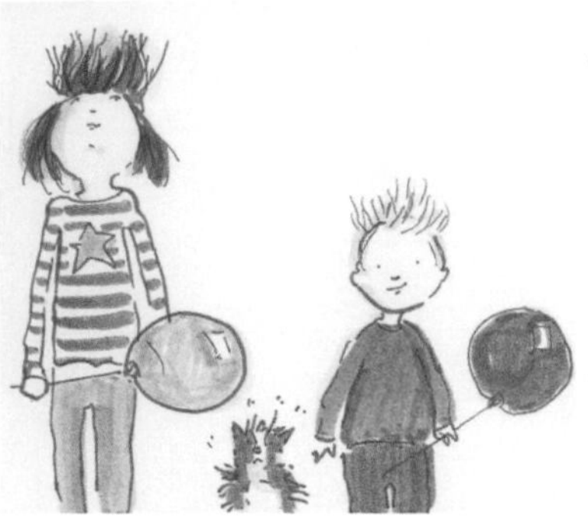

Fun and Games

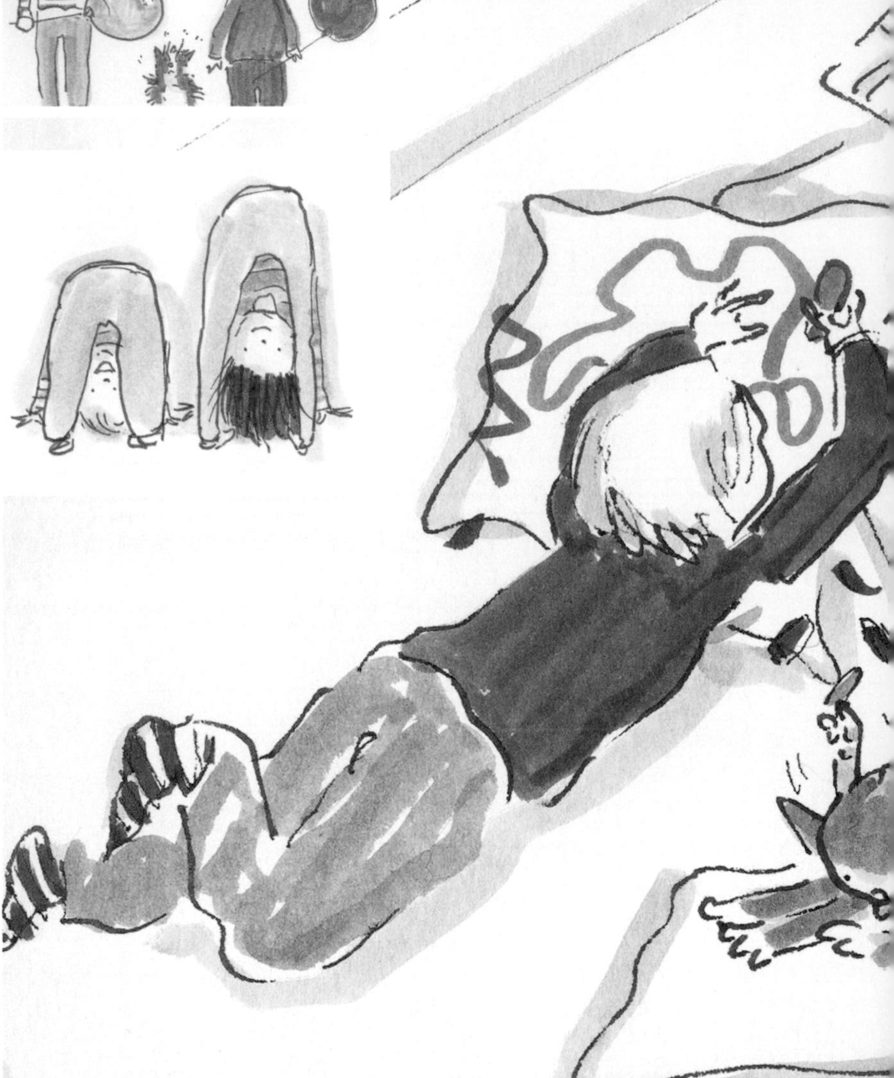

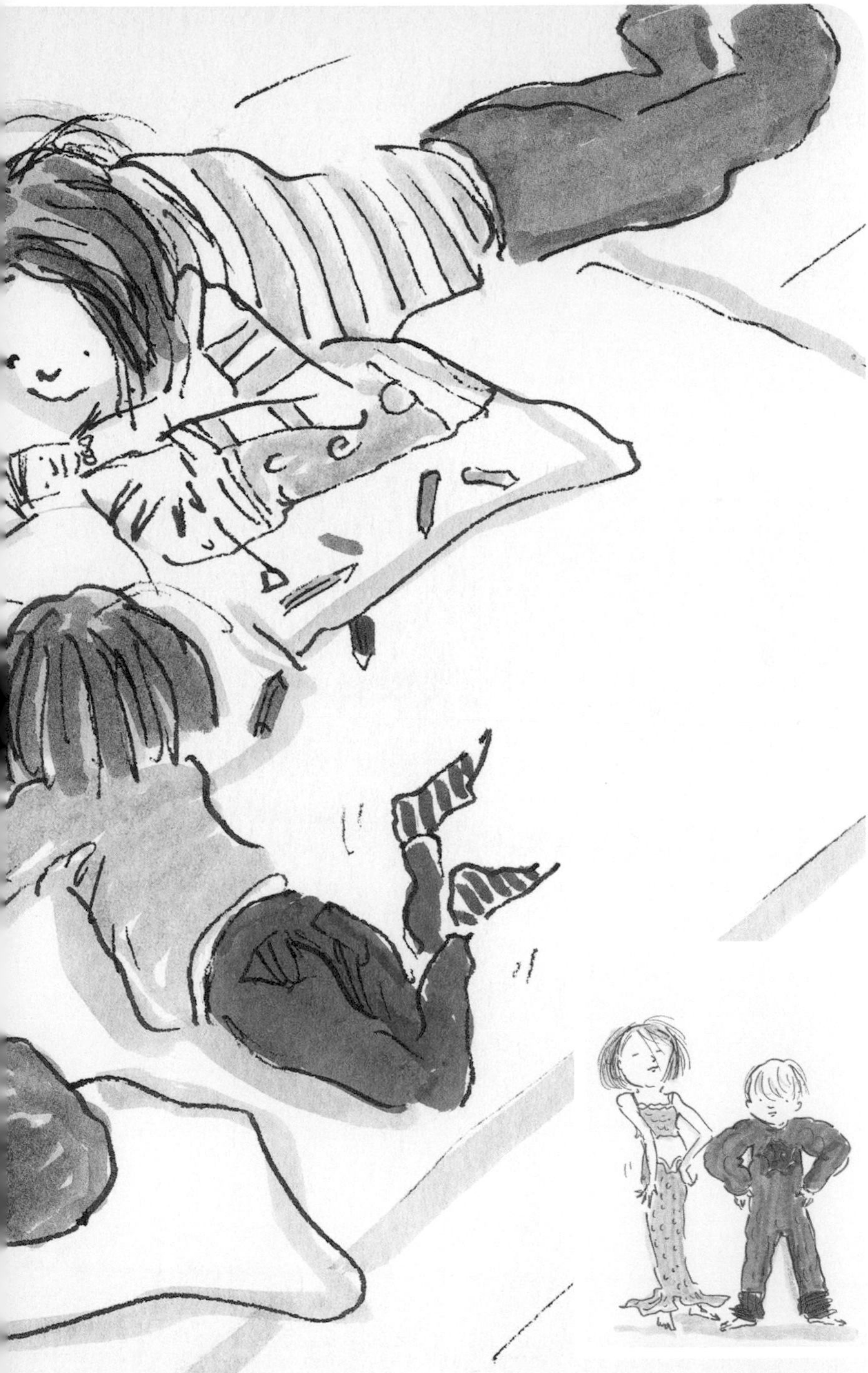

there's nothing good to play with in this house...

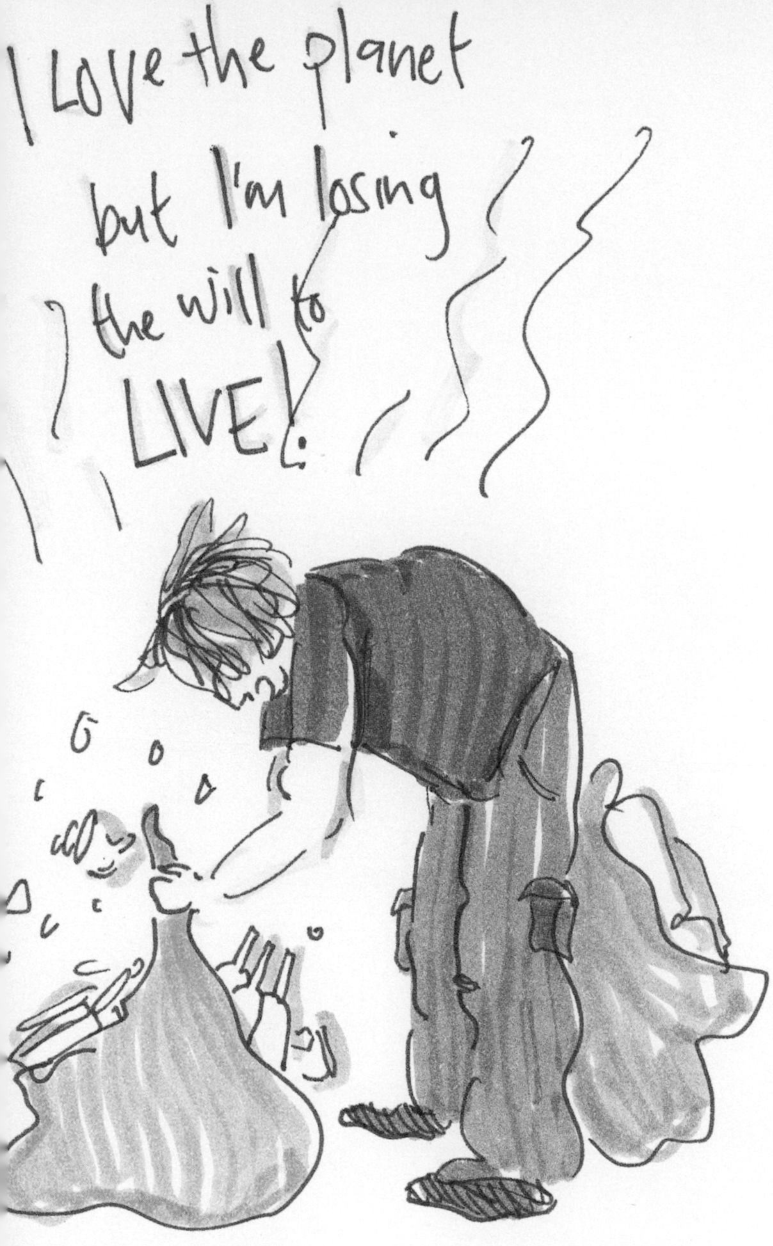
I love the planet
but I'm losing
the will to
LIVE!

June

warm sun, bare toes and grass - bliss

Pooh sticks in the river, who will win?

bubbles and dandelions...

...blow your wishes into the sky

Evie's dino-garden of little monsters

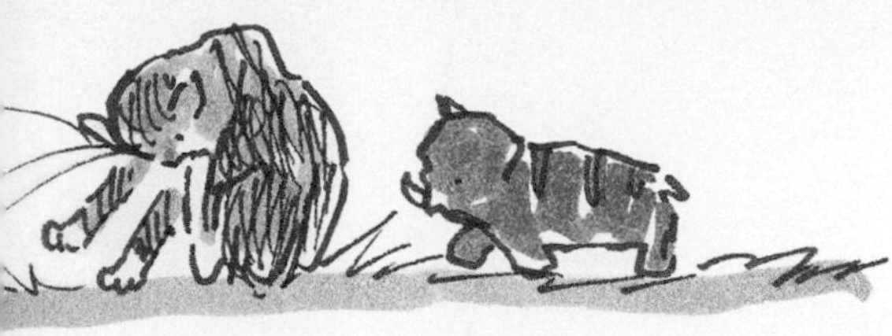

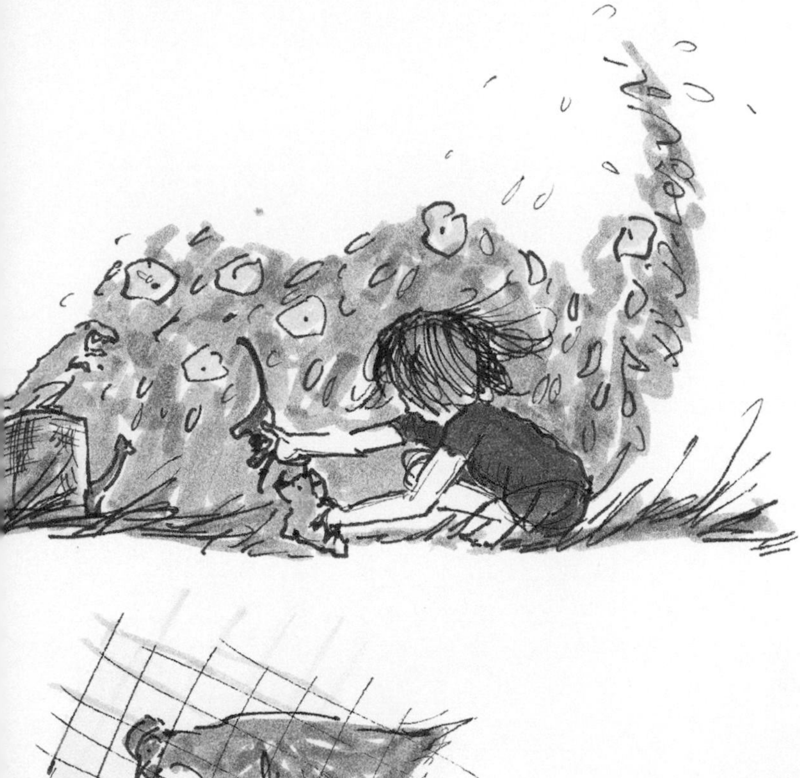

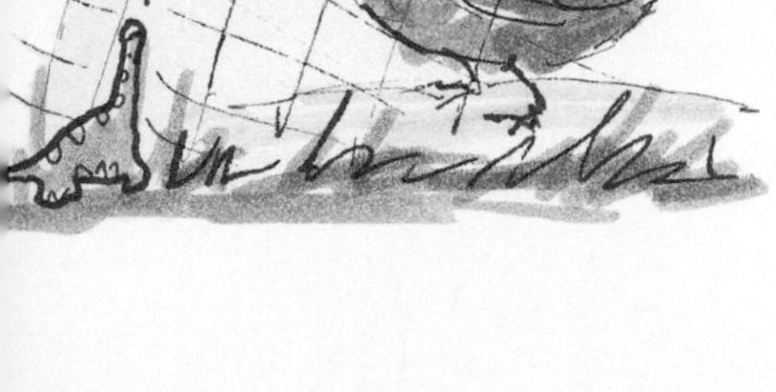

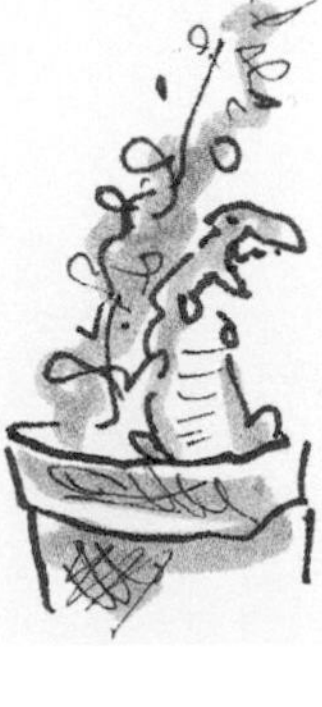

their Daddy is a big, scary, hairy, Viking.

(on weekends only of course)

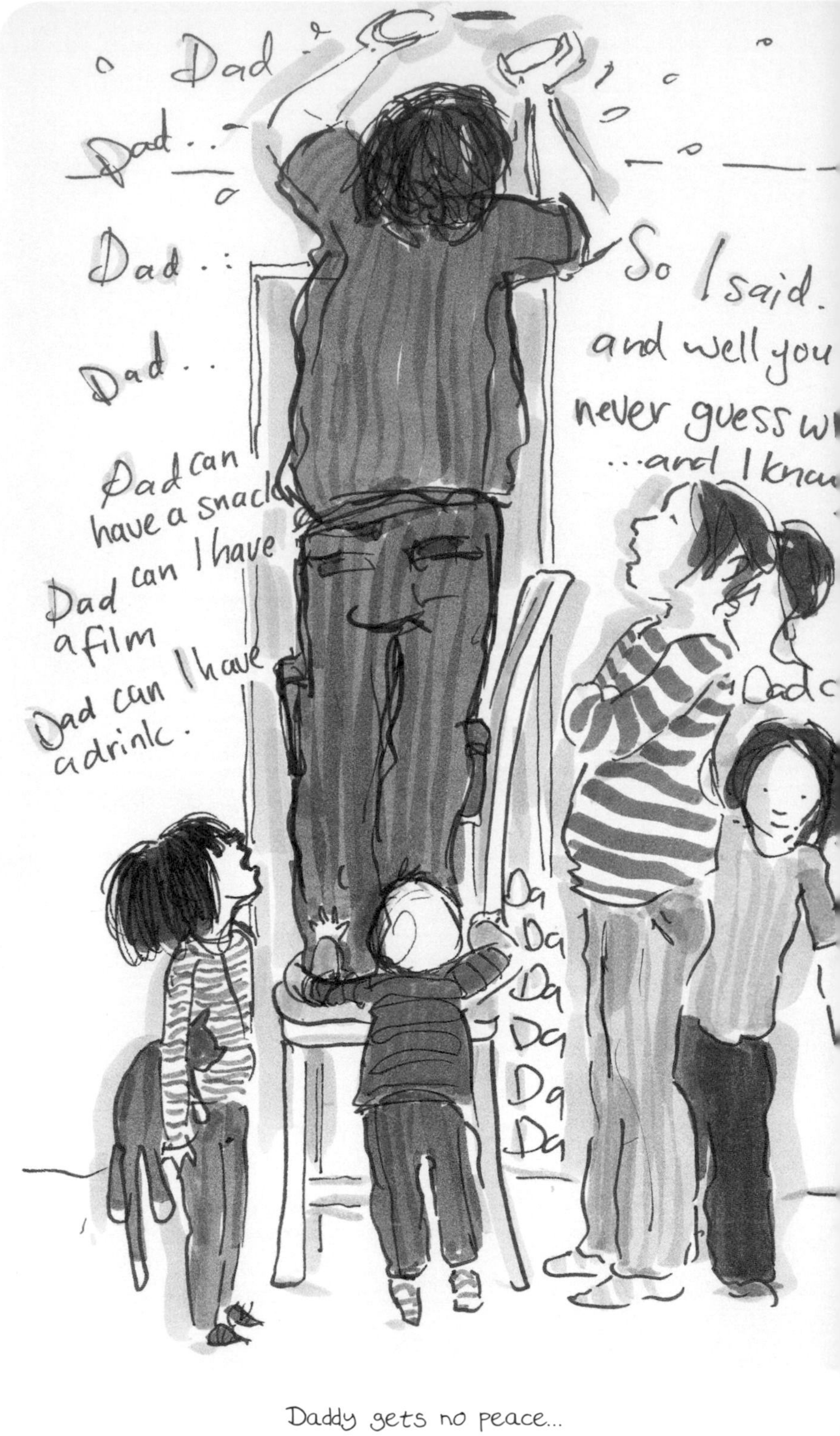

Dad
Dad...
Dad...
Dad...
Dad can have a snack
Dad can I have a film
Dad can I have a drink.
So I said.
and well you never guess wh
...and I knew
Dad c
Da
Da
Da
Da
Da
Da

Daddy gets no peace...

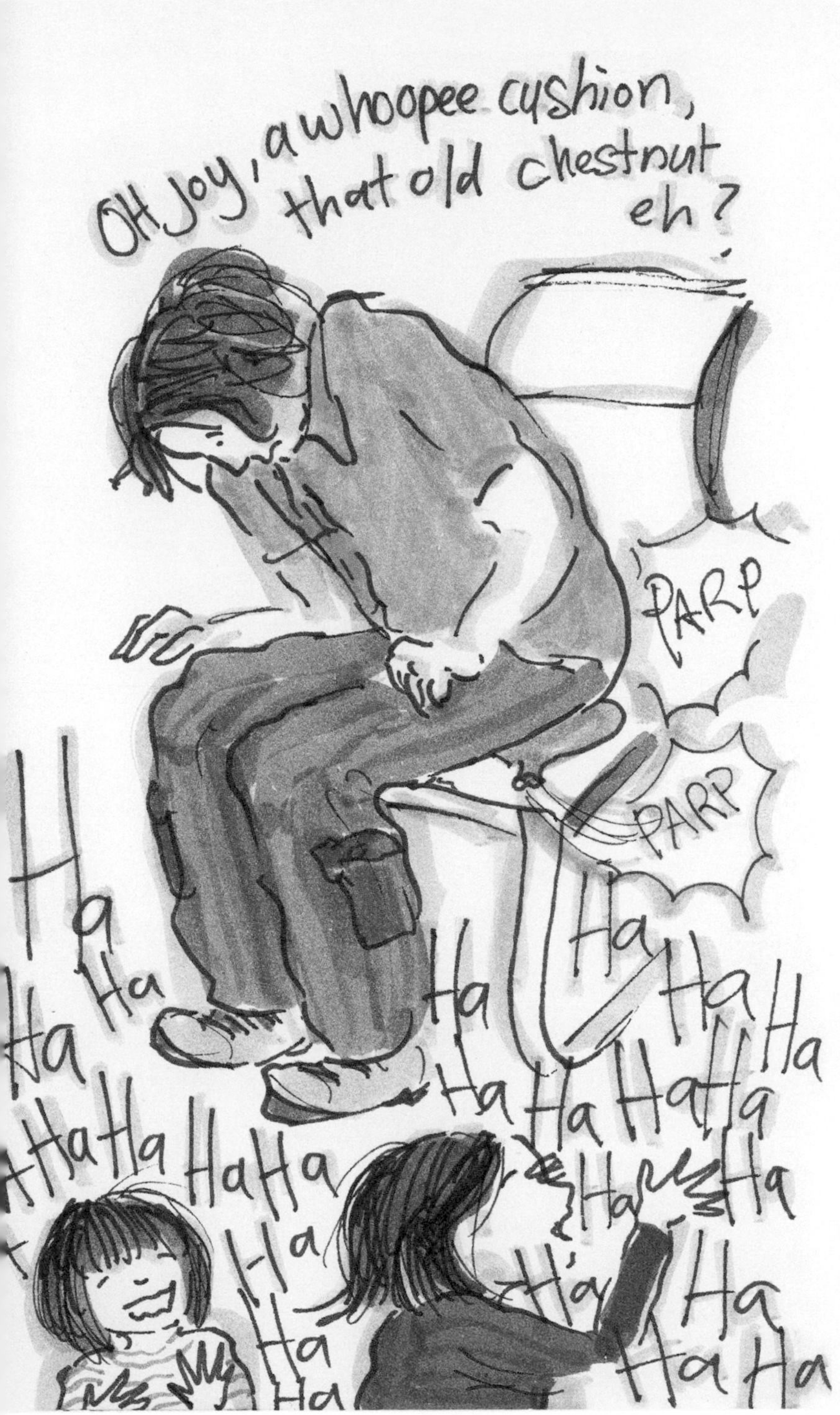
OH joy, a whoopee cushion, that old chestnut eh?
PARP
PARP
Ha Ha Ha Ha Ha Ha Ha Ha Ha Ha Ha Ha Ha Ha Ha Ha Ha Ha Ha Ha Ha Ha Ha Ha Ha Ha Ha Ha

...or quiet!

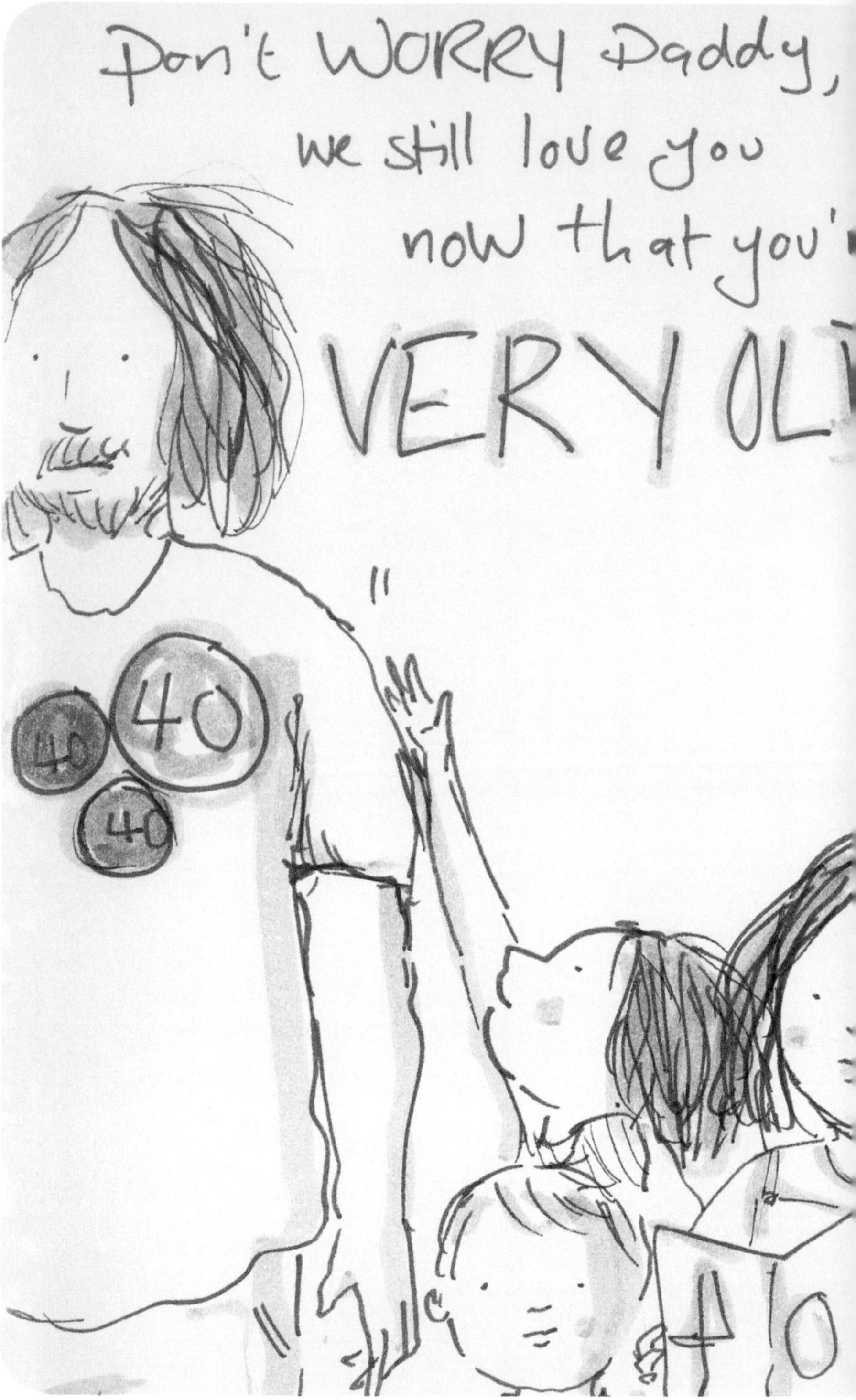
Don't WORRY Daddy,
we still love you
now that you'
VERY OL
40
40
40
40

Happy Birthday old man!

July

school's out!

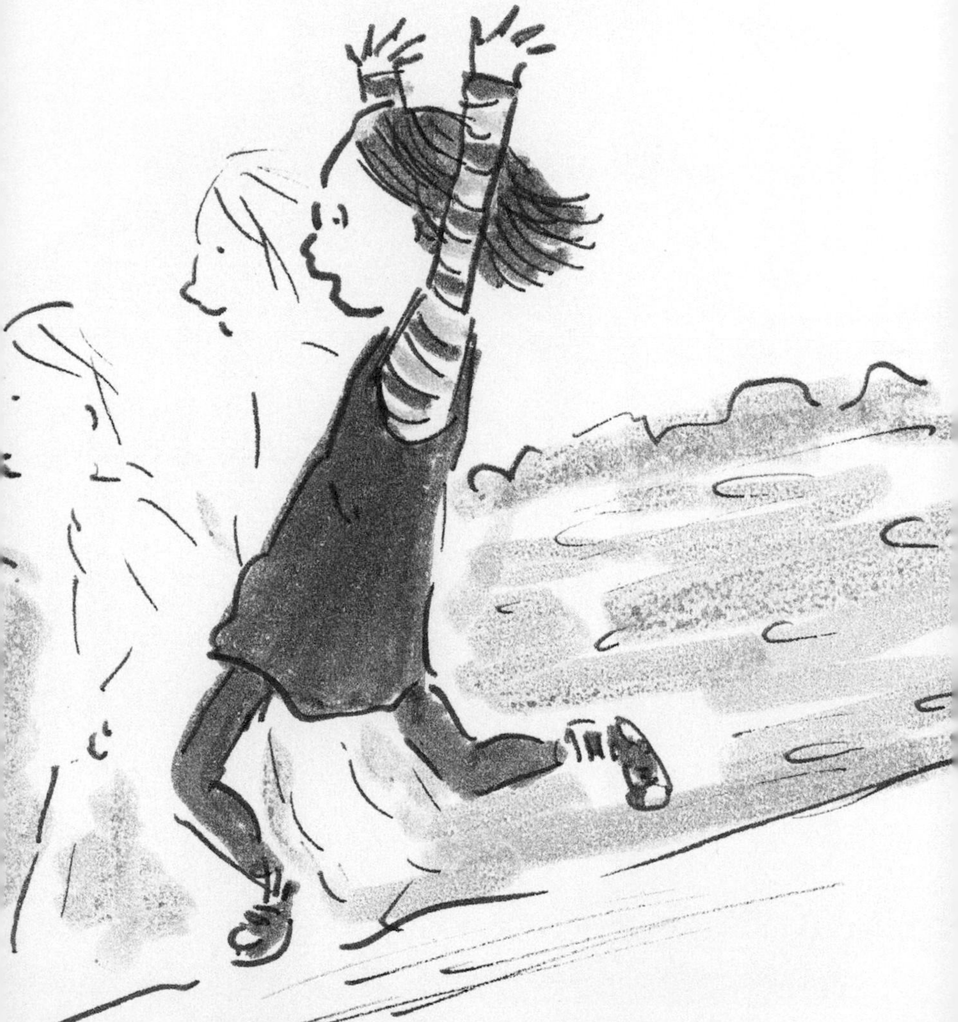

Adventures in Messiness

Adventures in Vacuuming

Sports Day Fun

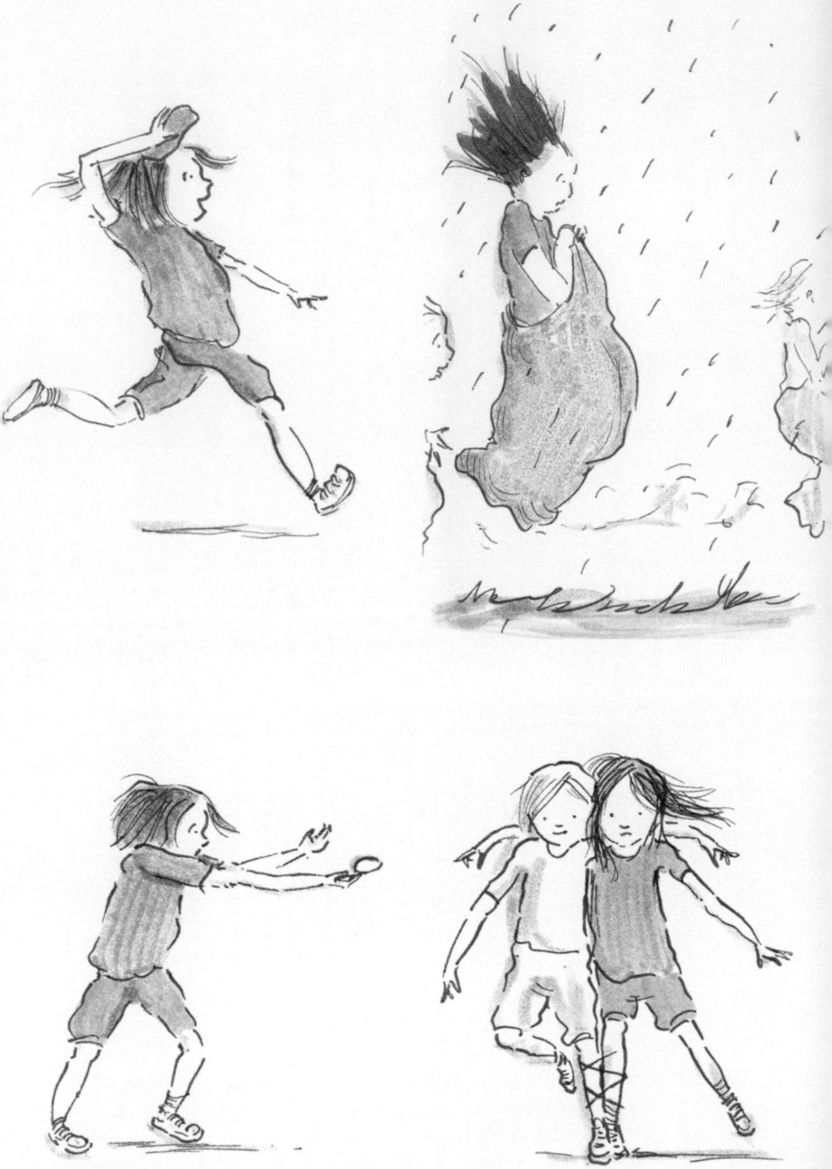

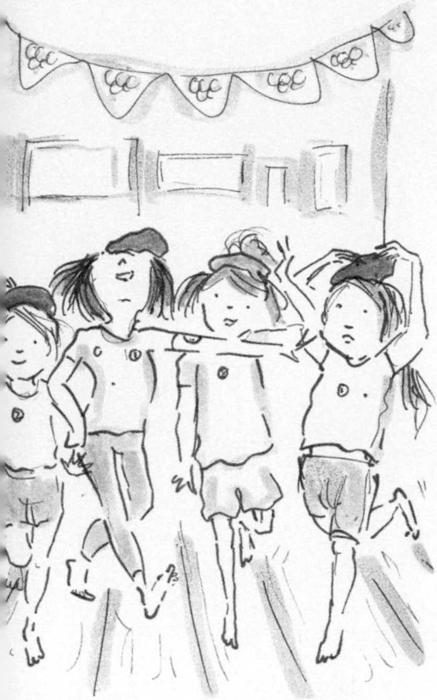

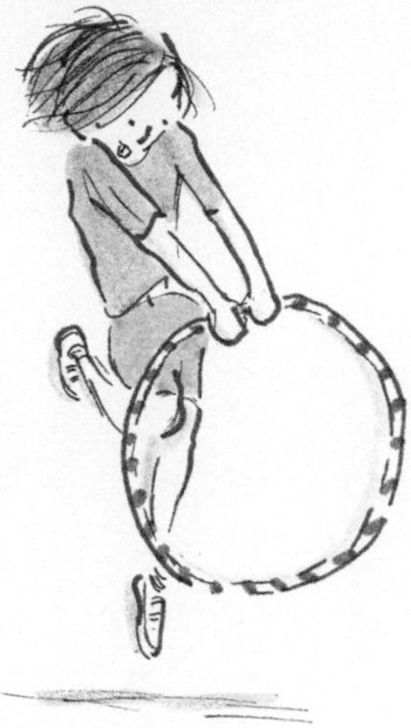

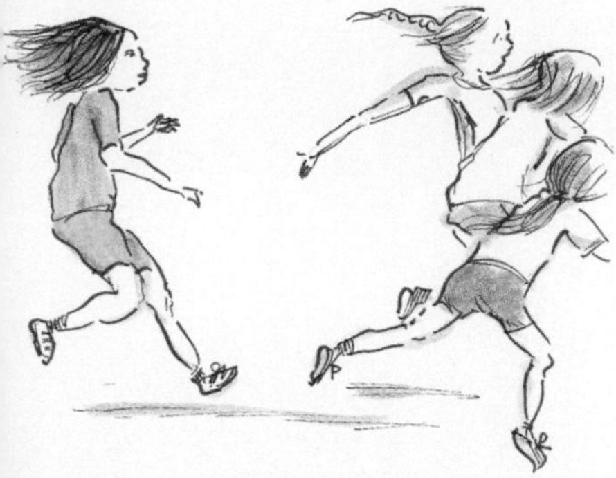

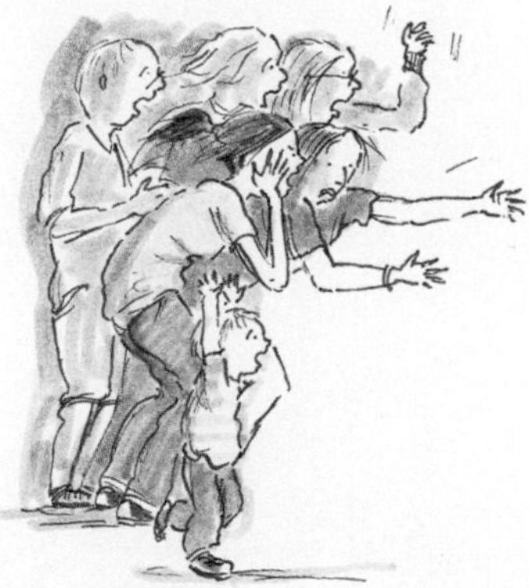

There's a WORM at the
bottom of the garden,
and his name is...
WIGGLY WOO

Wiggly Woo

the sun's out and so is the mower...

run while you can kids, I'm armed and gloopy...

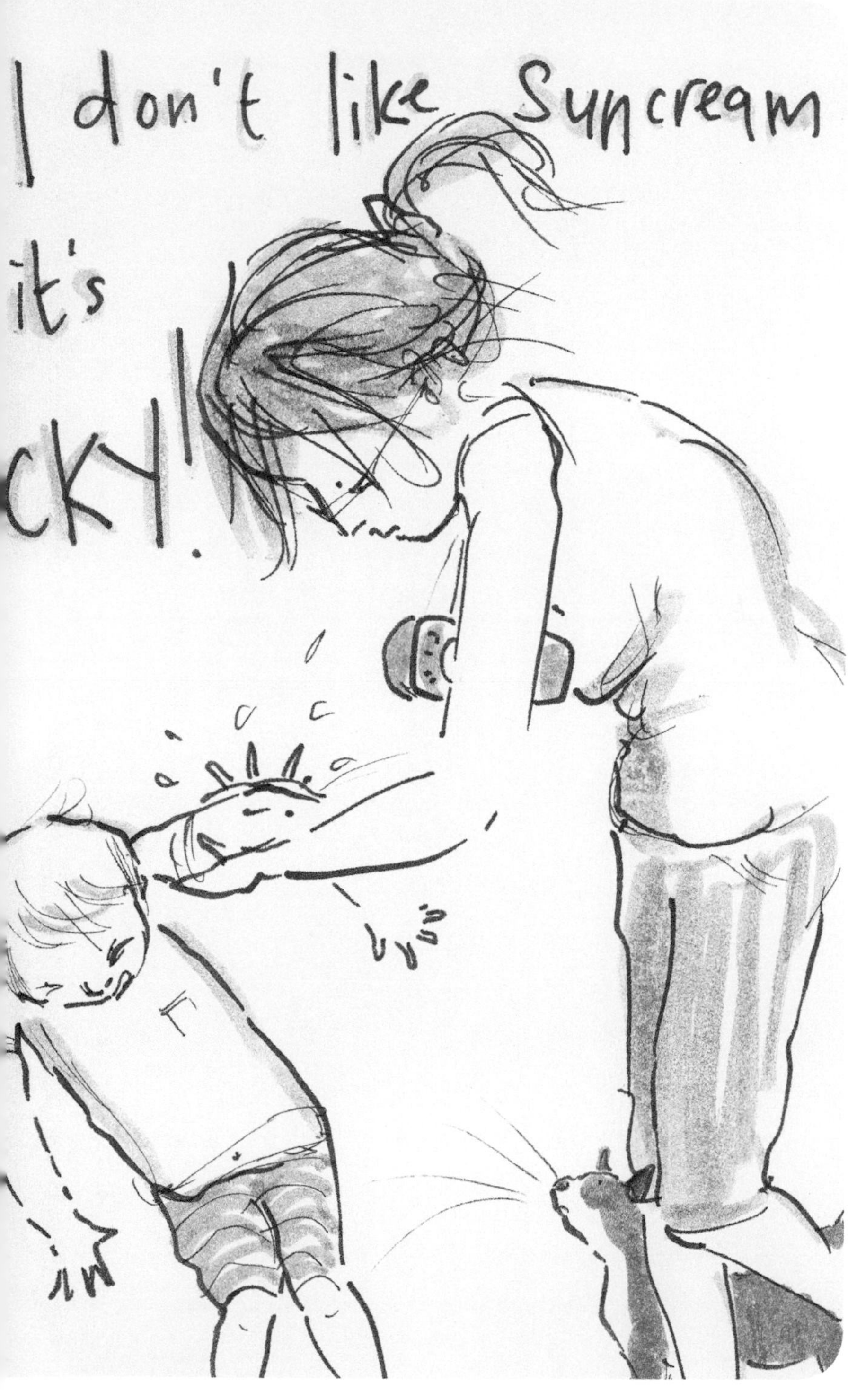
I don't like Suncream
it's
CKY!!

an awfully big beach adventure...

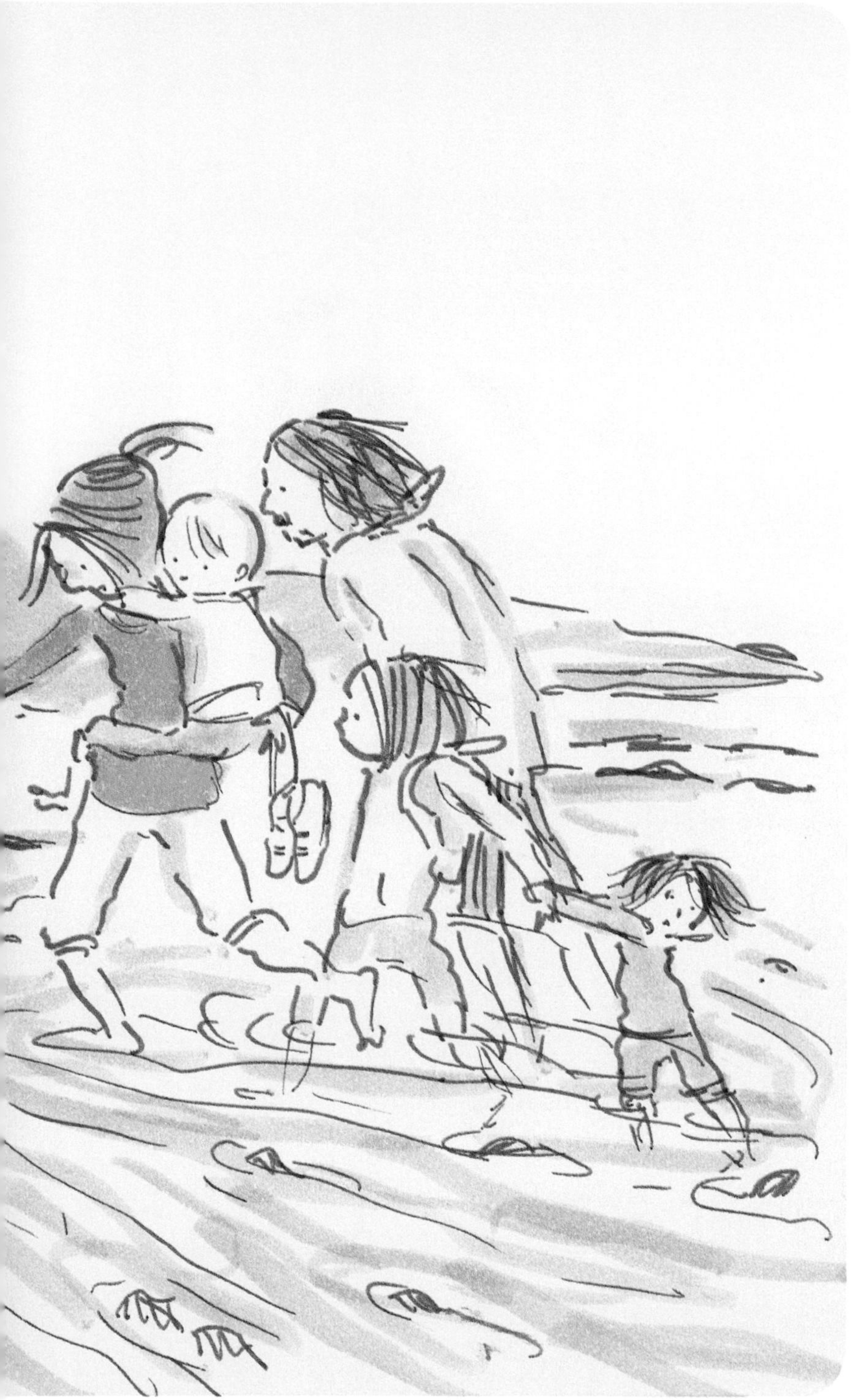

a sand mermaid with seaweed hair

we all scream for ice cream!

August
camping, mud &
great big adventures

A Year of Washing

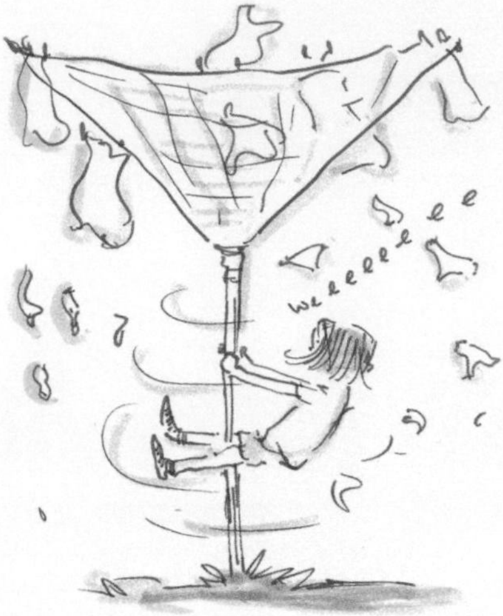

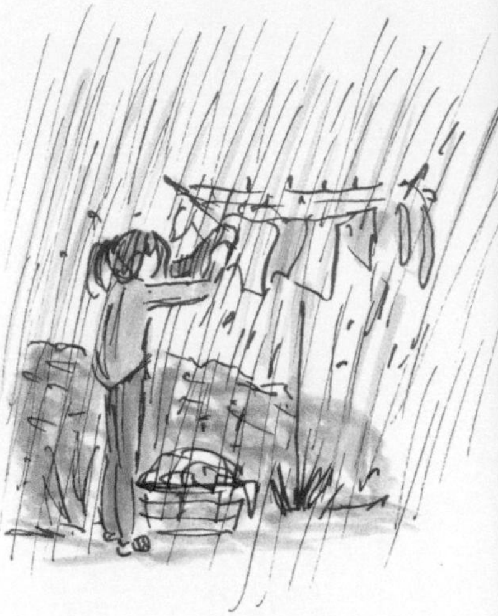

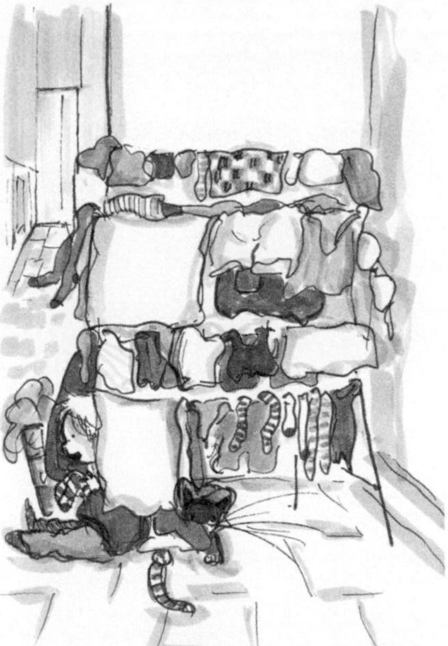

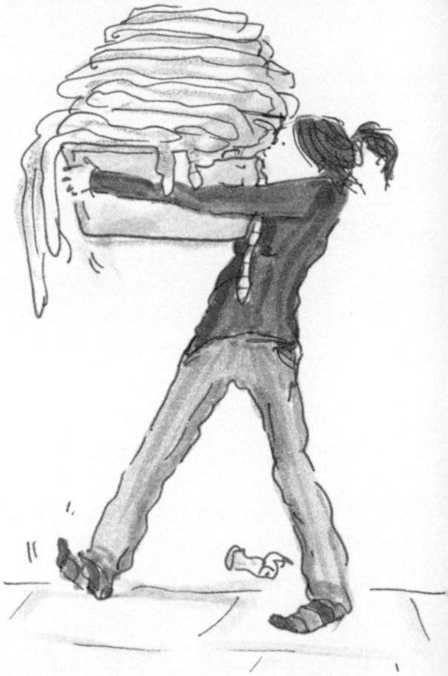

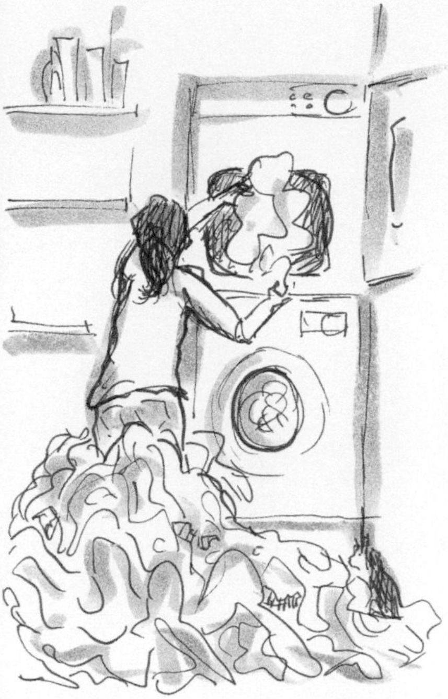

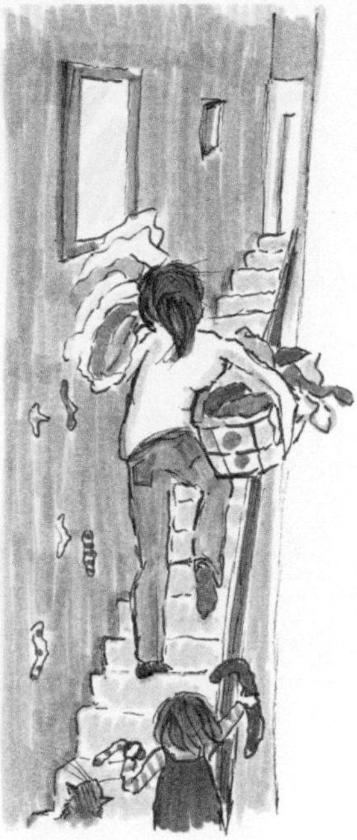

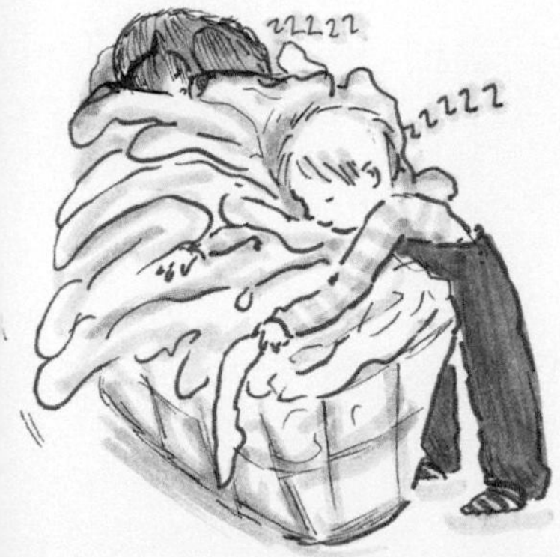
zzzzz
zzzzz

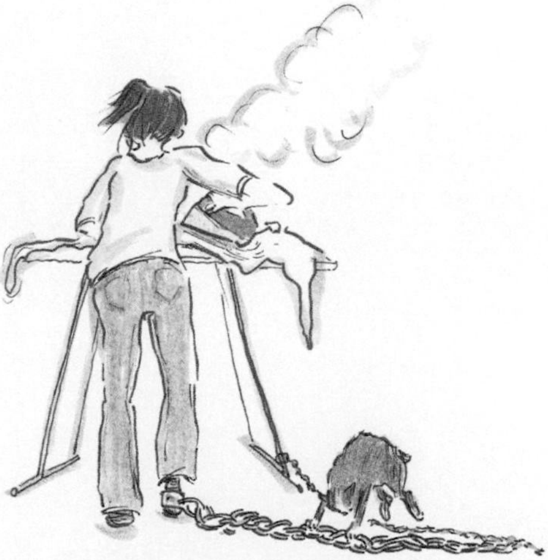

packing (the house) for our big camping adventure -

ALL my dinosaurs
and my
mermaid
costumes

My axe
my car
an' my wo wo.

ALL of my DOCTOR WHO
comics

Four books.
and all my PALEKS.

kitchen sink not included..

a relaxing, peaceful camping holiday, toy guns optional...

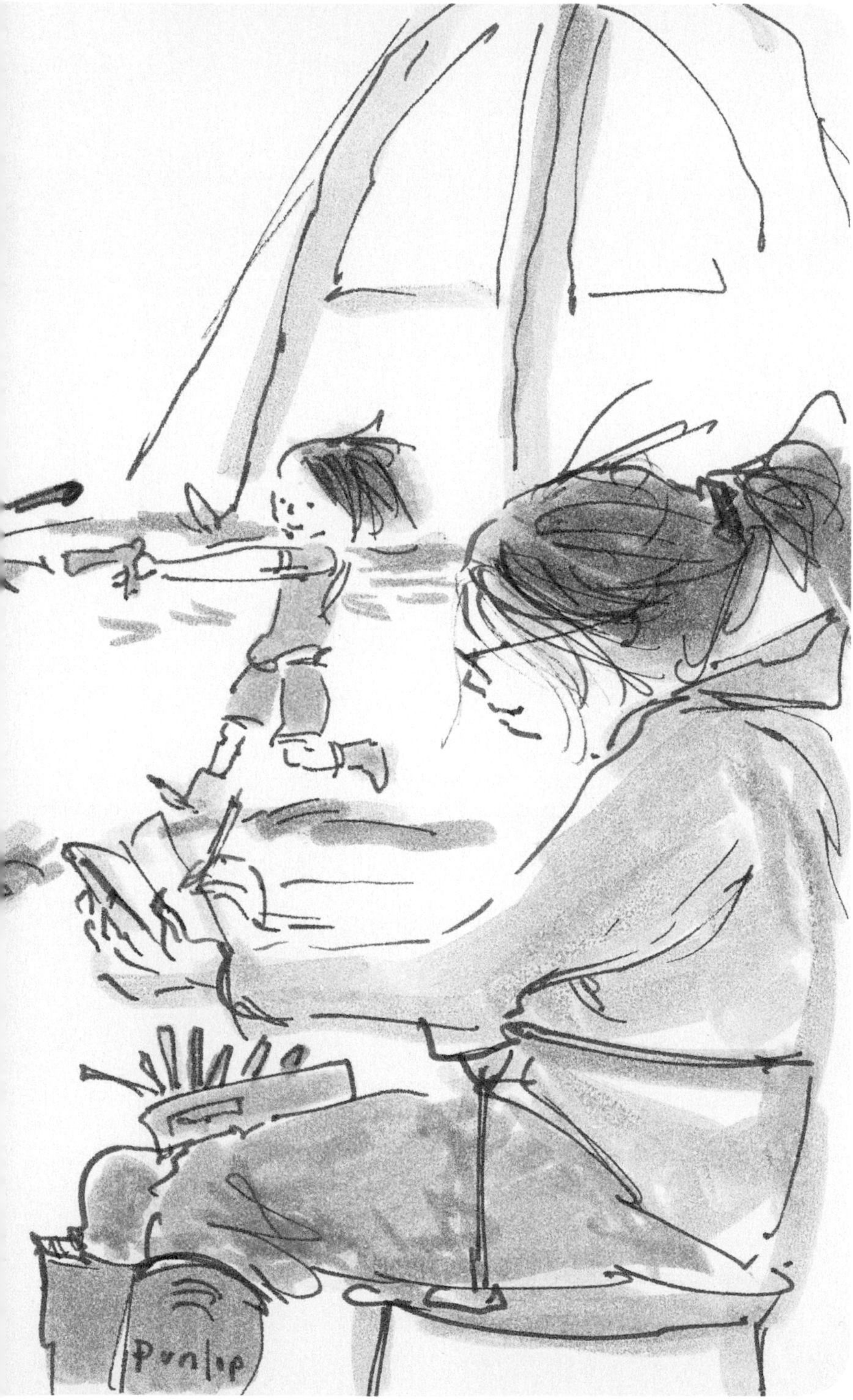
Dunlop

make your own entertainment...

...but beware of those tent monsters

princesses actually like castles, Evie...

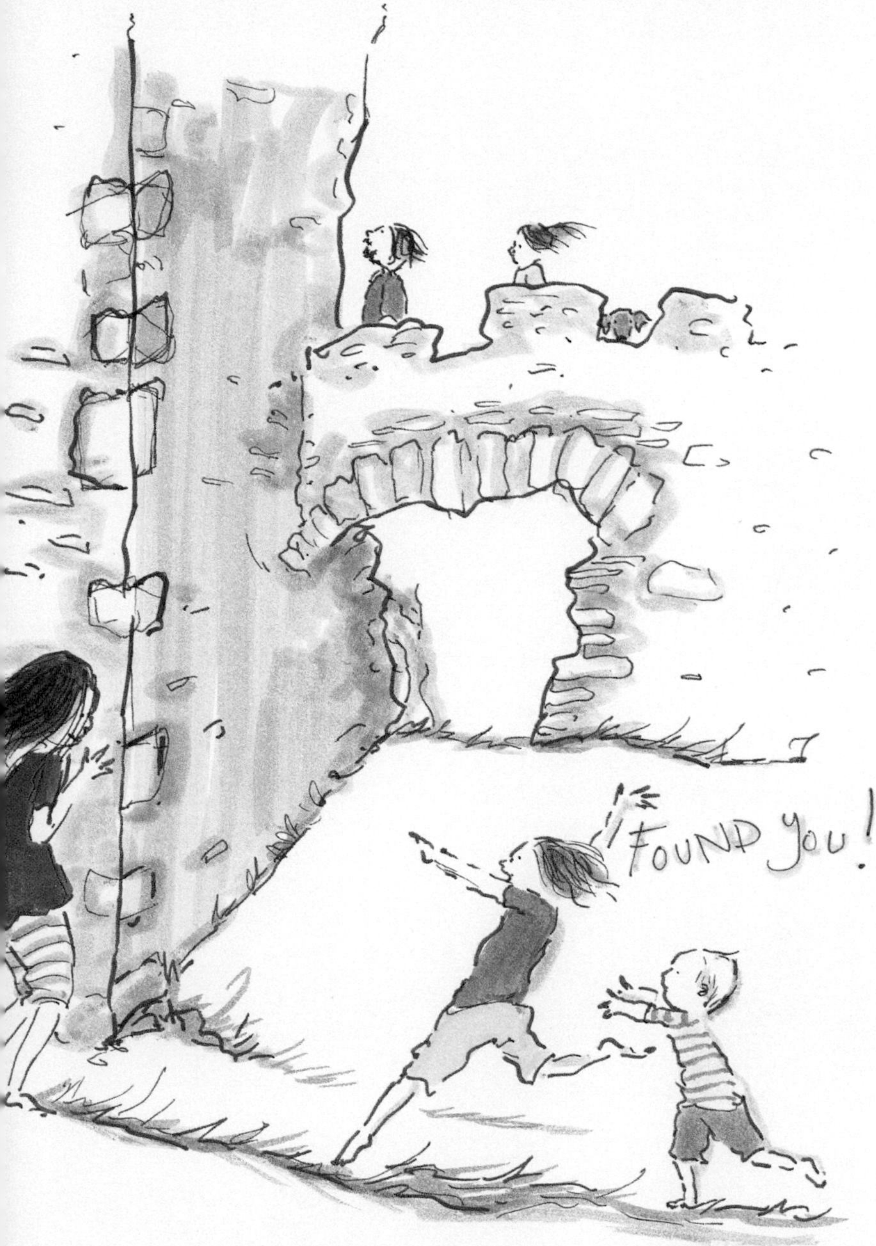
FOUND YOU!

ah the great British music festival, never complete without mud...

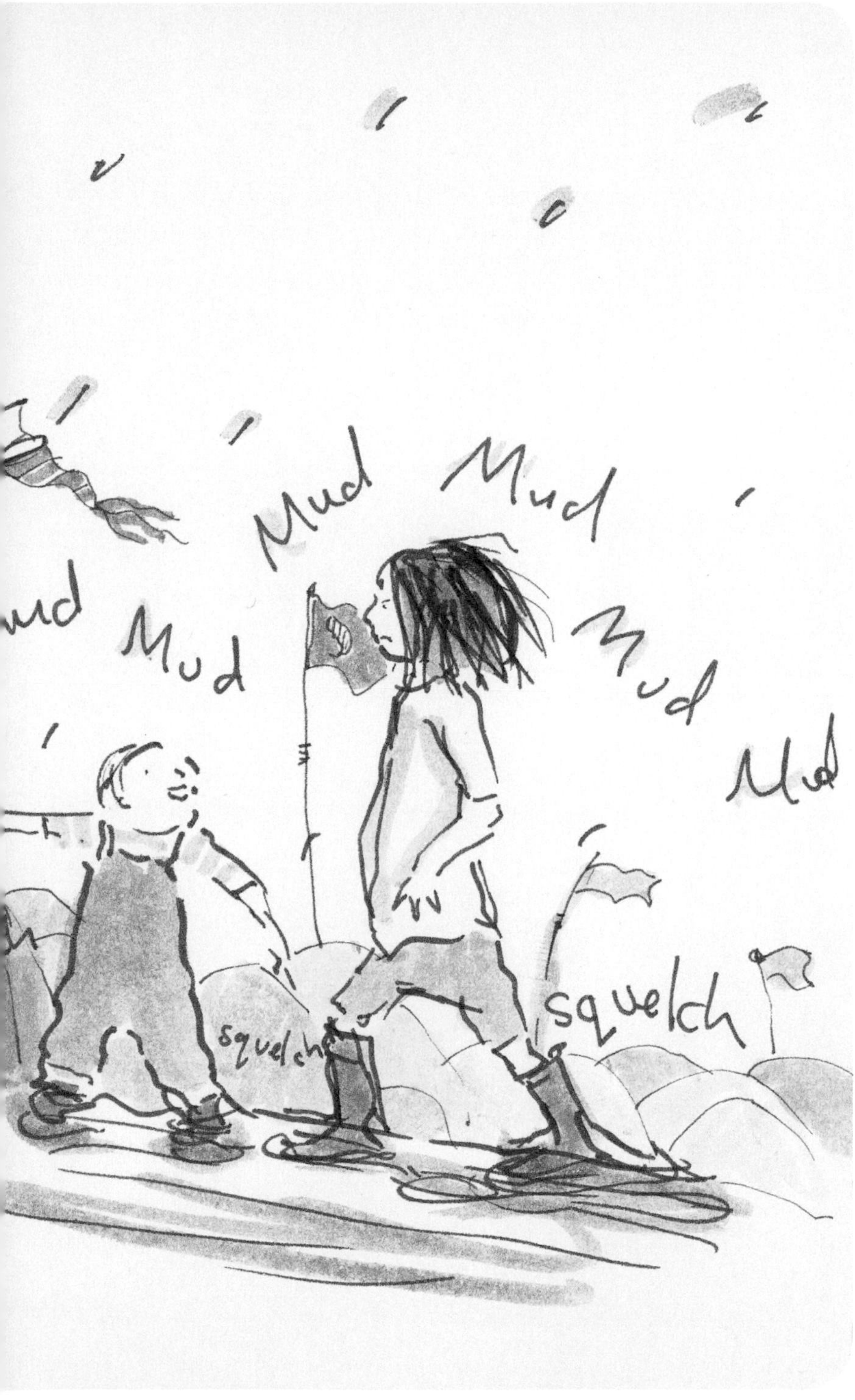
Mud
Mud
ud
Mud
Mud
Mud
squelch
squelch

...lots of mud...

...and did I mention the rain...lots of rain....

September

back to school

I don't think they're REALLY rocket powered...

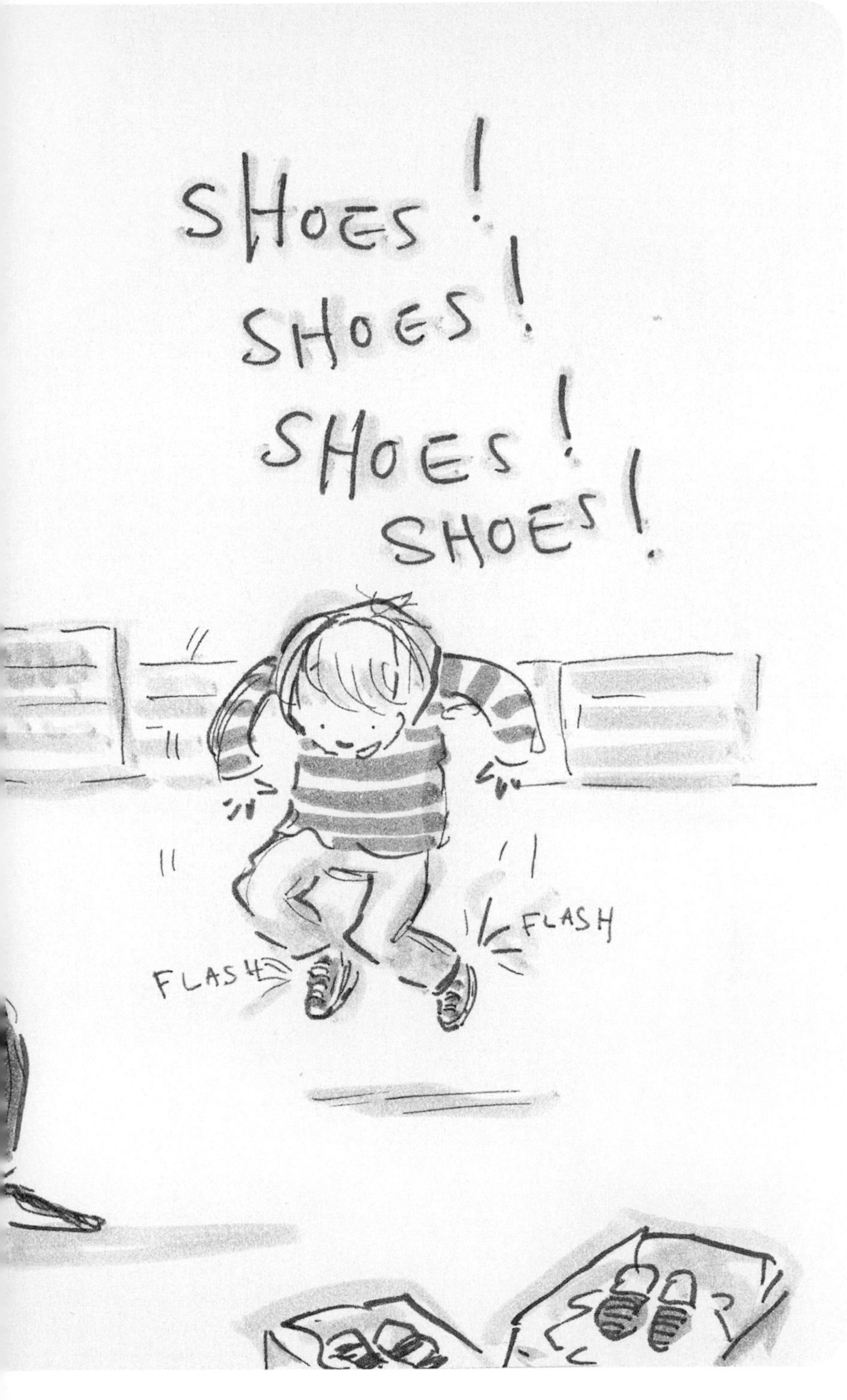
SHOES!
SHOES!
SHOES!
SHOES!
FLASH
FLASH

morning little piggies

who's afraid of the big, bad brush?

my Monday morning mantra

e you got your lunch?
coat on....
got your shoes on...
1R coat on...
ou got yaw shoes on...
T YOUR COAT ON....
oh for...
Millie.... Millie.... turn the
tv off.....
Gruff...get yOUR....
" COAT ON...._Right
GO.·GO..GO

first day back at school - miss you already...

and a blow by blow acount of the day

autumn is a time of squirrel hunts

best of all though - conkers!

not best of all at all though - spiders (biders)

October

witches, parties and
big dinosaur cakes

soggy, wet, cold trudges to school and back

~~Four~~ more sleeps

~~Three~~ more sleeps

two more sleeps

till my

Dinosaur Party

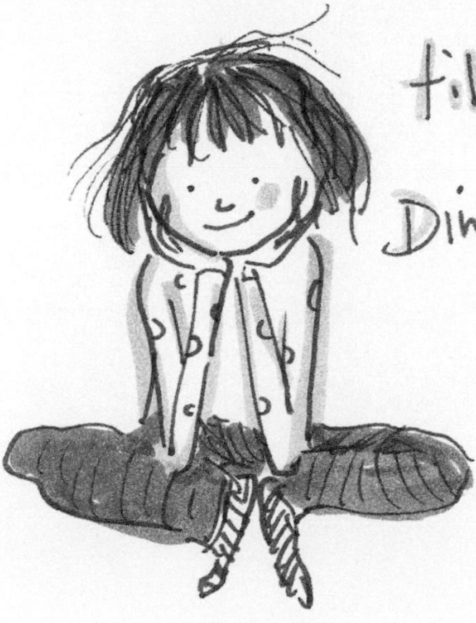

someone's having a birthday and someone wants a dinosaur cake...

let party preparations begin!

lots of wrapping paper and half a kilometre of
carefully placed sticky tape should do it...

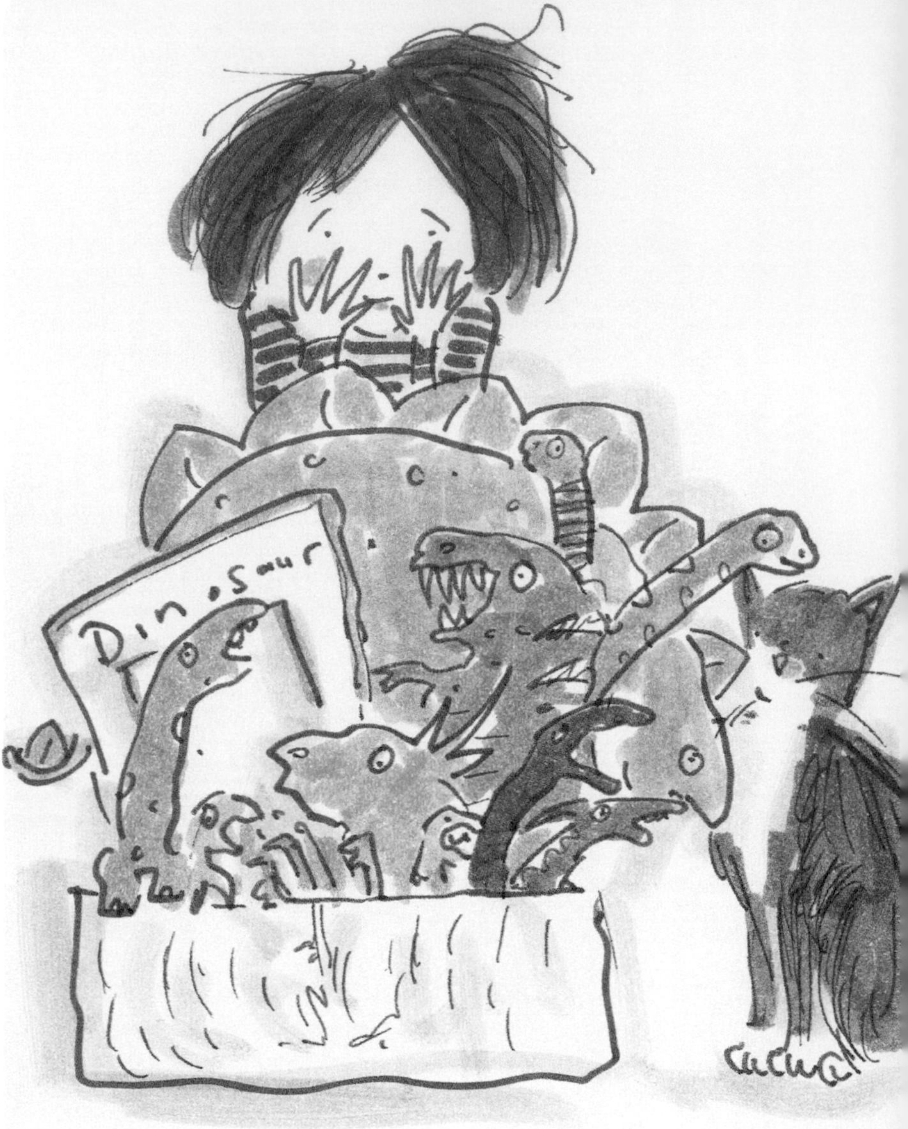
Dinosaur

dinosaurs? for me?

time to blow up the balloons - deep breath Evie!

Myles 'loves' doing the drinks...

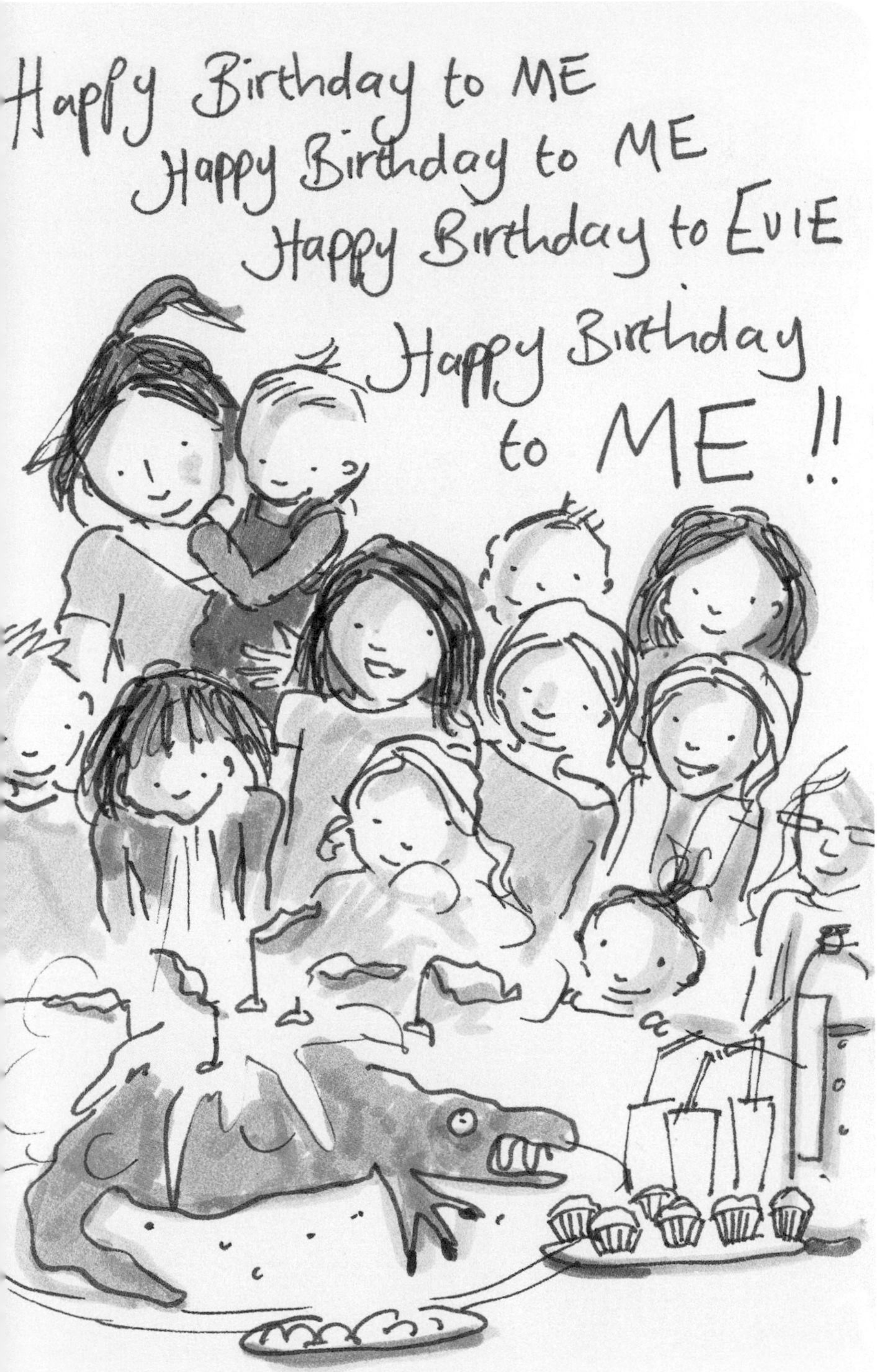
Happy Birthday to ME
Happy Birthday to ME
Happy Birthday to EVIE
Happy Birthday
to ME!!

witches and monsters and lots of spider webs

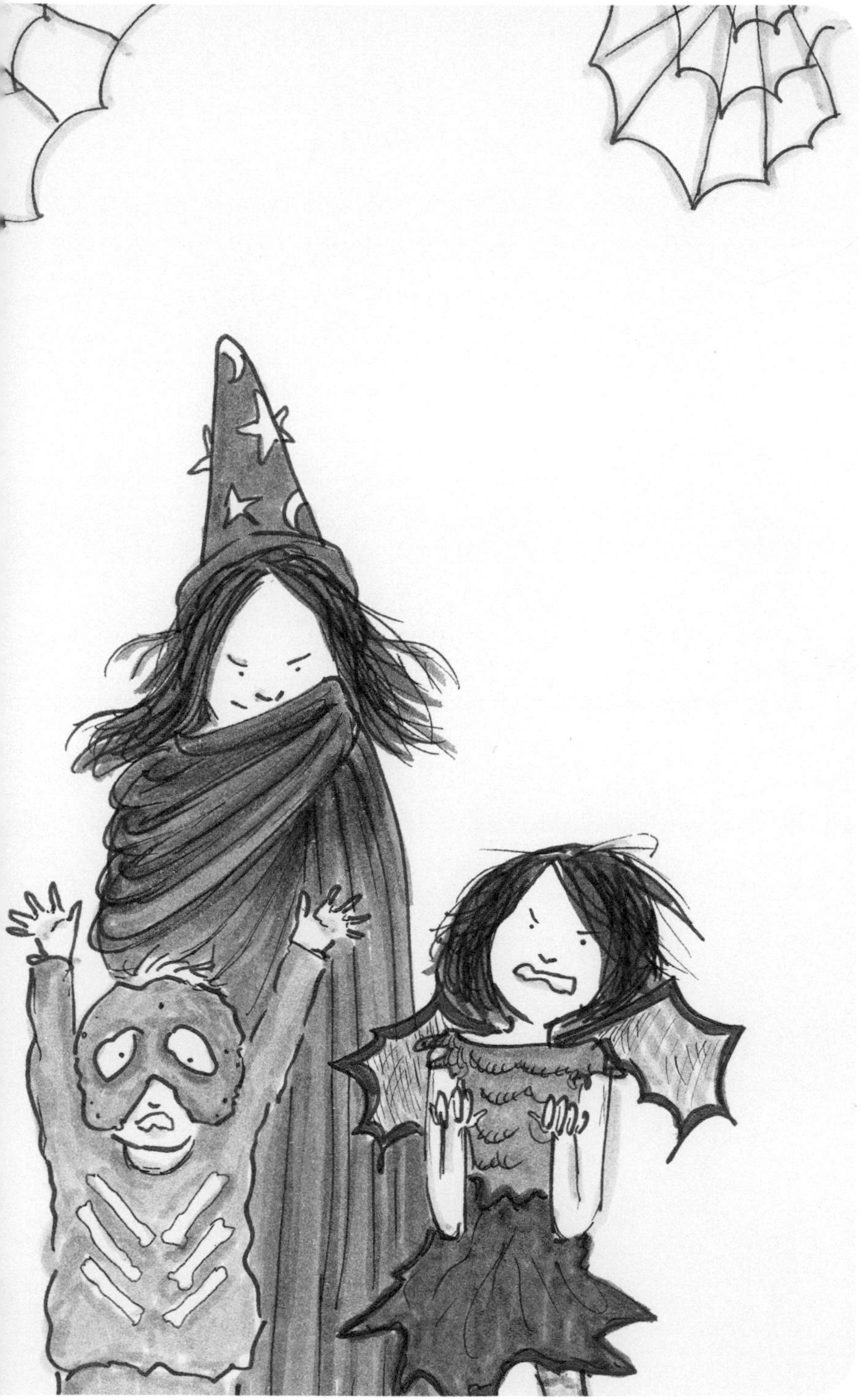

trick or treat?

Animals

what would our house be without animals? (cleaner)

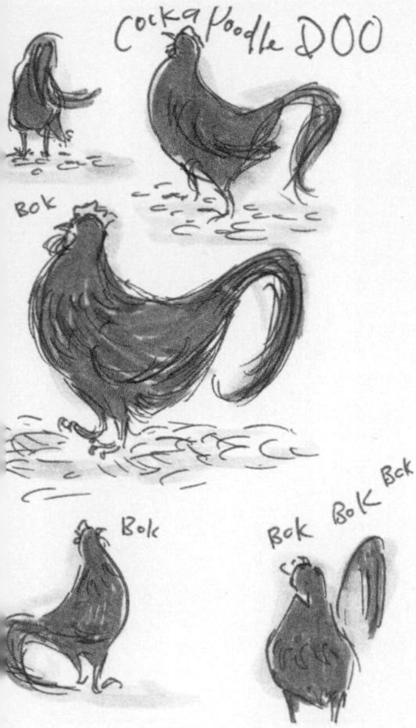
CockaDoodle DOO
Bok
Bok
Bok Bok Bok
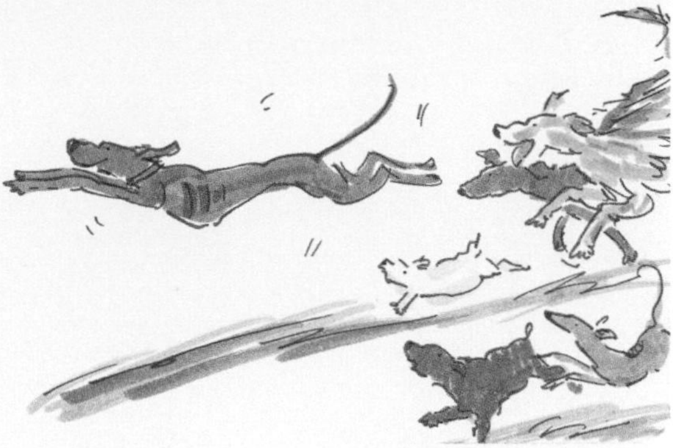
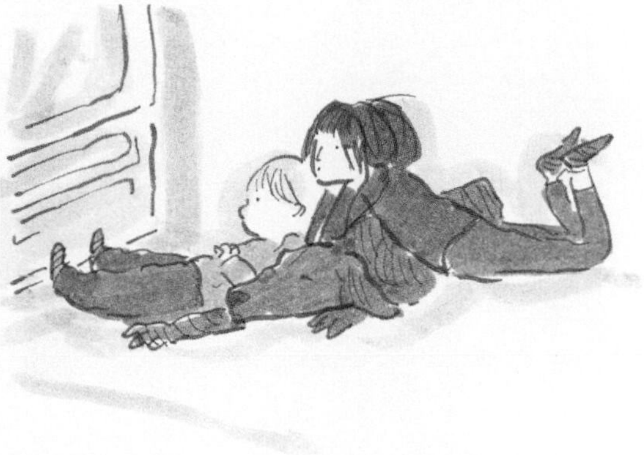
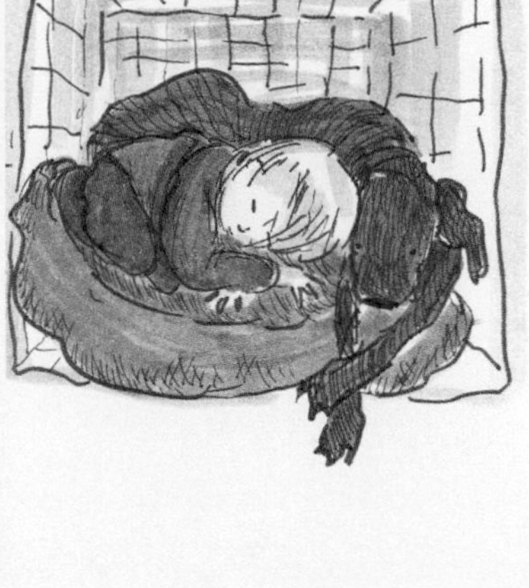
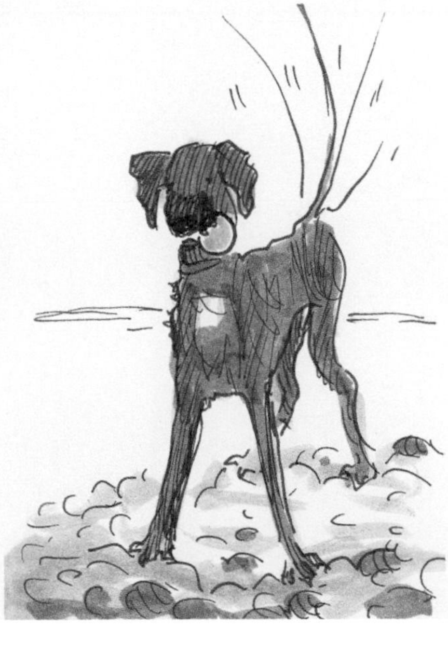

When I'm in bed and
the moon is out.
I see your face in it.
'And I think it's lovely
And I go to sleep.

Evie.

November

noisy, messy mayhem

oh hello – good night was it Bonnie?

Mummy's been knitting again, maybe some eye holes in your hat Gruff...

Happy Birthday rocket boy

a sword, a shield and a mighty doggy steed

welcome to our Artistic Academy of Art and Music

MAM! I think Gruff has got your COLOURS and he's Coloured his HEAD!

I am a ROBOT

I am a ROBOT

I am a ROBO

if I'd just bought Gruff a box for his birthday, he'd have been happ.

Some days, I would
just like to see
the floor.

wooooooooooooooo

it can't be Christmas yet, think I need to be speaking to Santa soon...

mber, it is not December
ng up to the loft yet.
:mber where I left
the decorations.
My Christmas
lights are
rubbish. I can't
afford to buy any
more.
HUMBUG

bonfire night, sparklers, and rockets - let me hear you say ooooooh...

December

Christmas is coming...

Advent Calendar

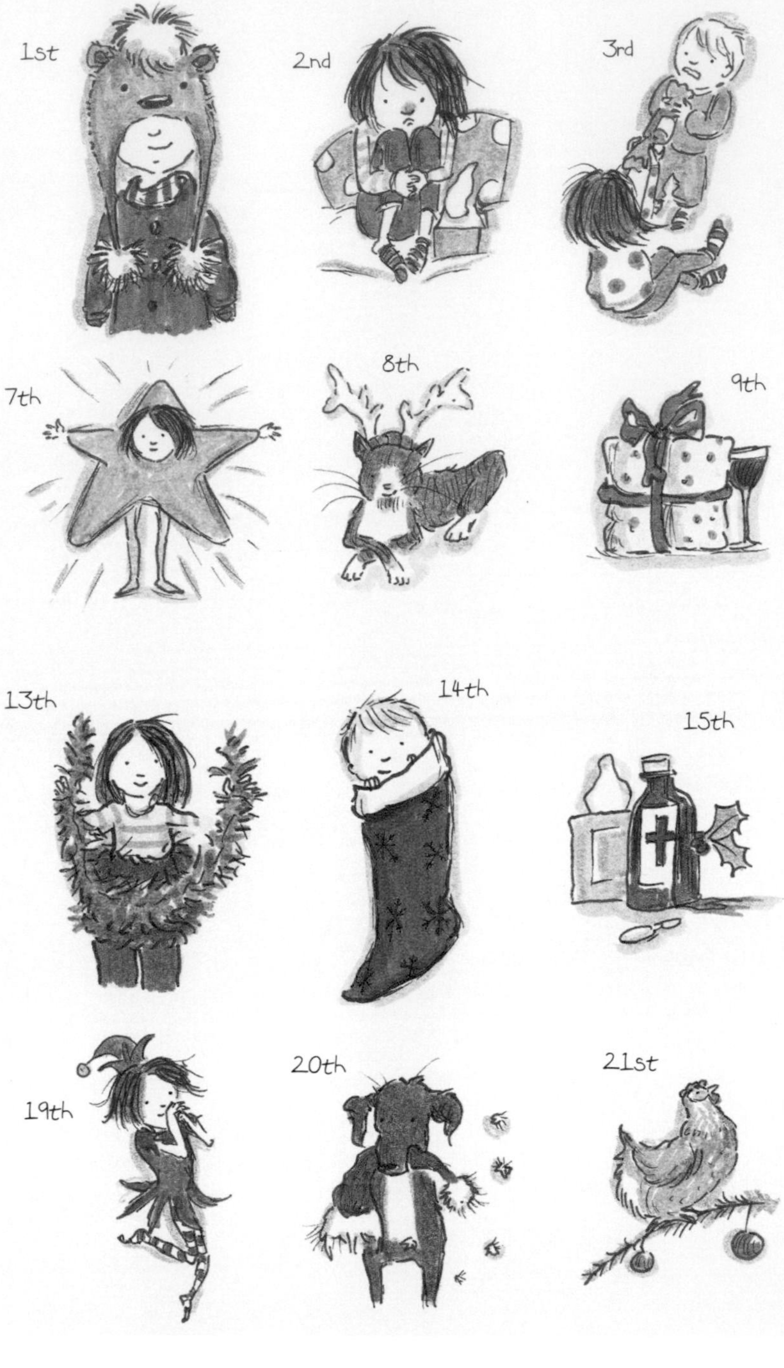
1st
2nd
3rd
7th
8th
9th
13th
14th
15th
19th
20th
21st

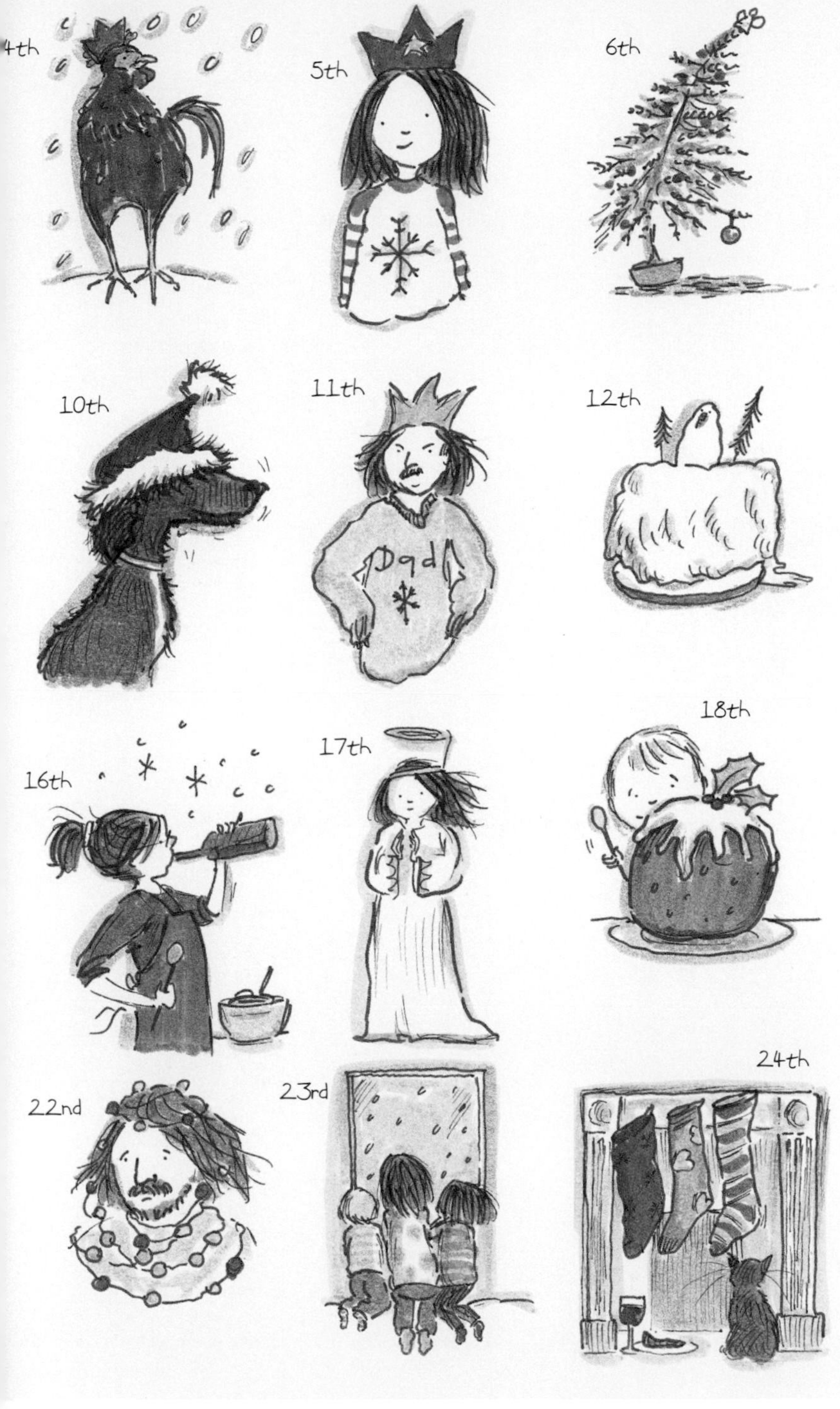
4th
5th
6th
10th
11th
Dad
12th
16th
17th
18th
22nd
23rd
24th

snow business - not for me!

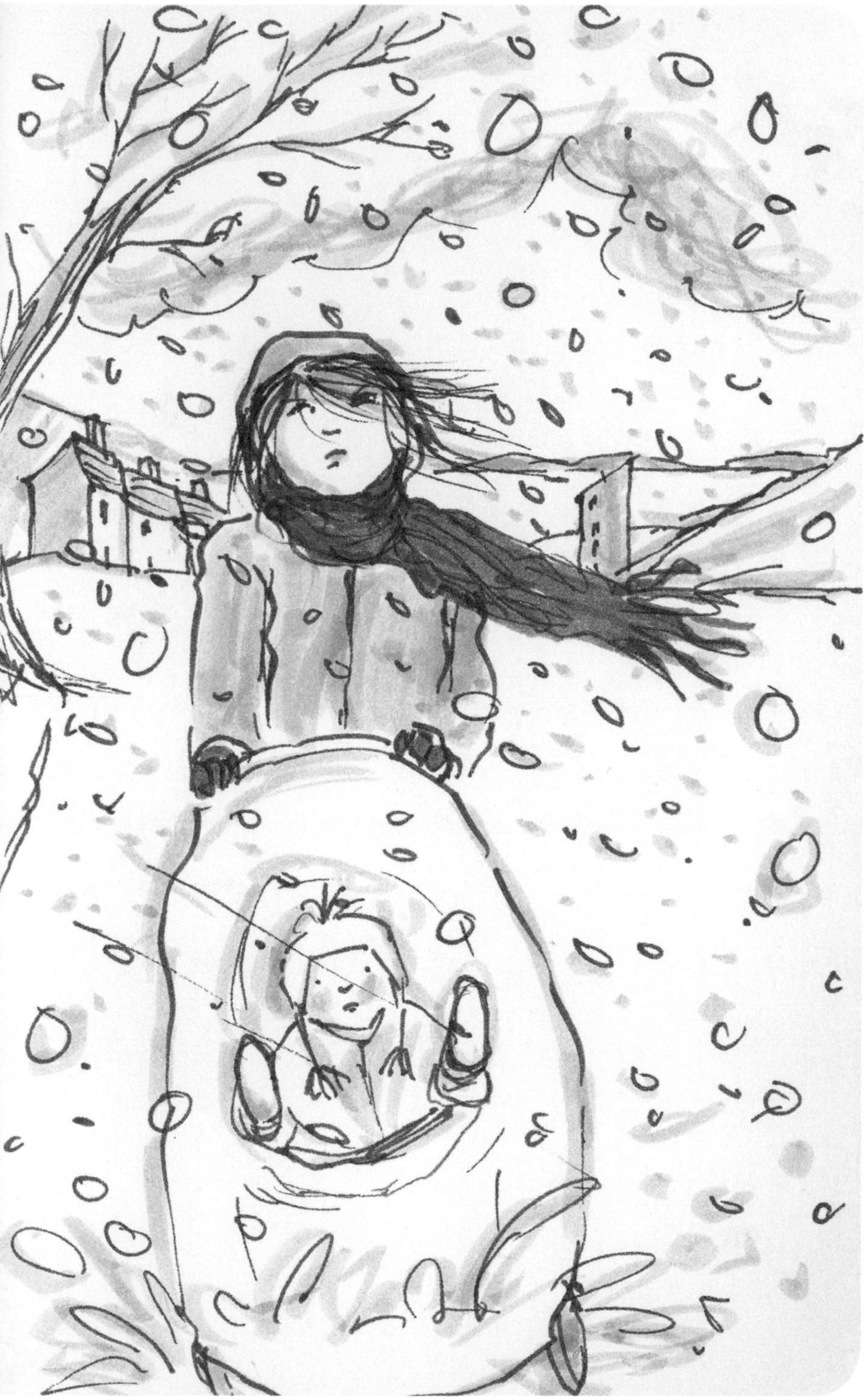

the Christmas concert - singing stars, cats & donkeys

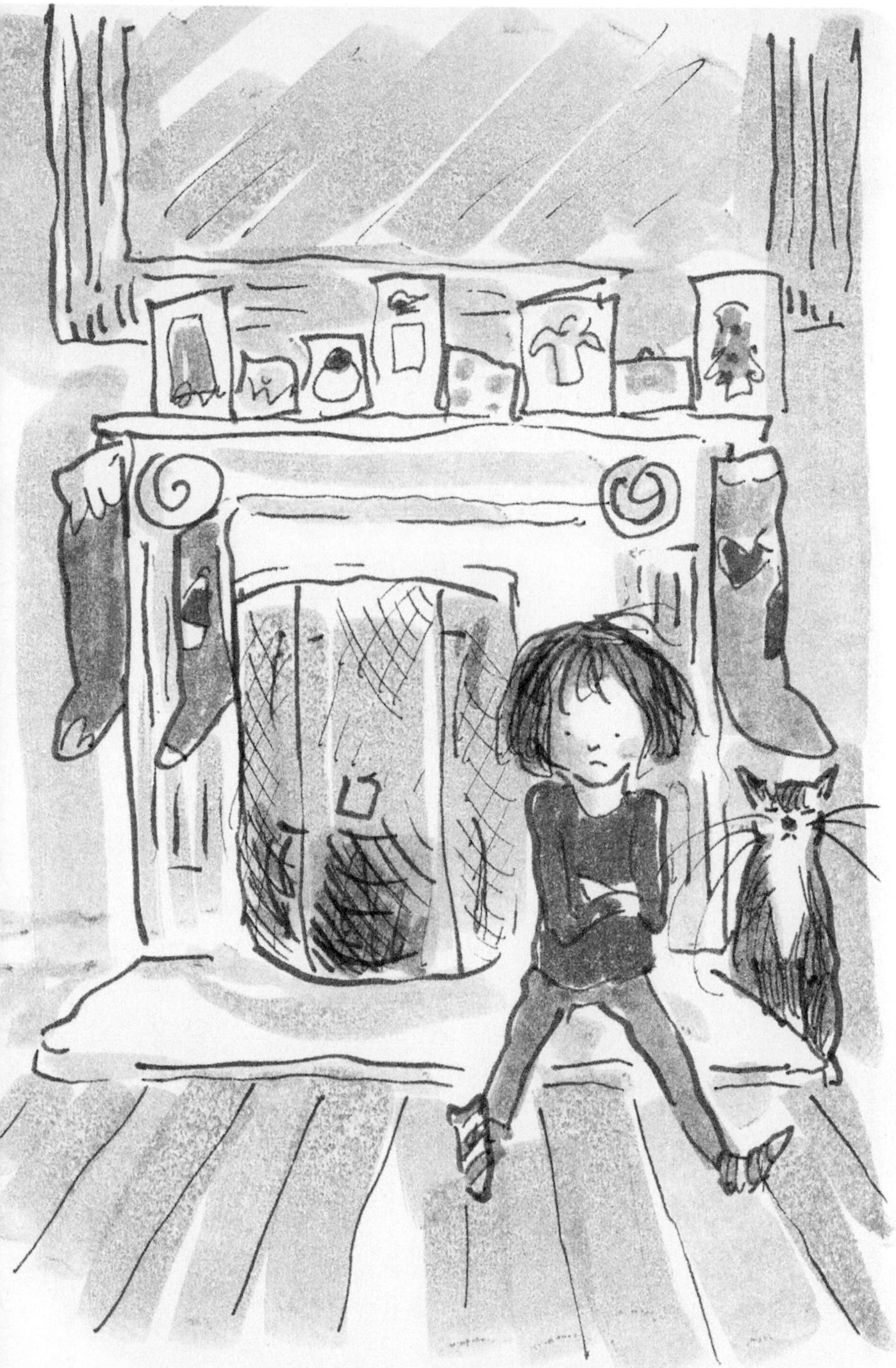

is it Christmas NOW?

decorating our tree just in time for...

...Mummy's birthday!

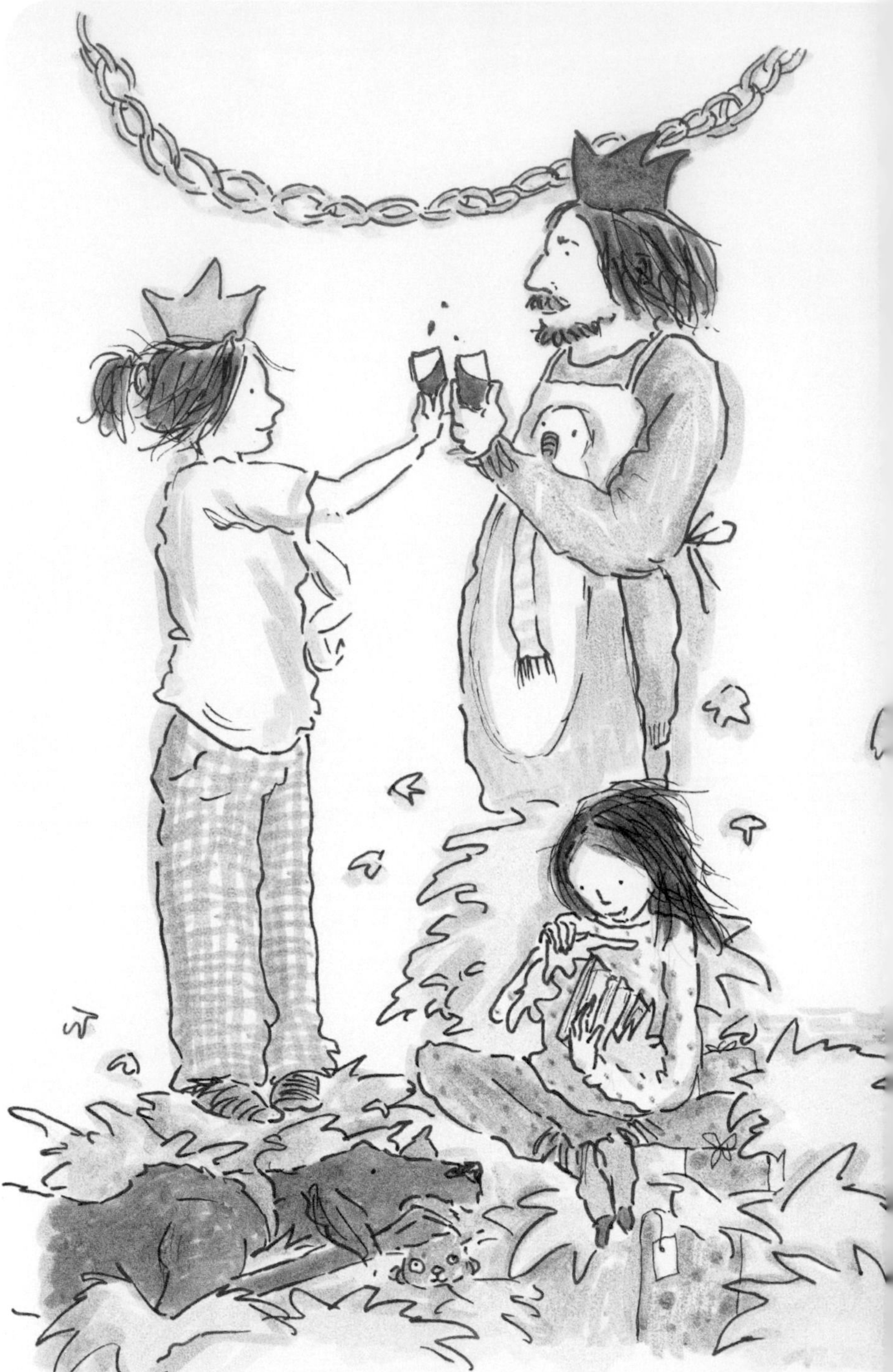

Happy Christmas

is it too early to open presents and drink sherry?

A Year of Family Hugs... and sleeping

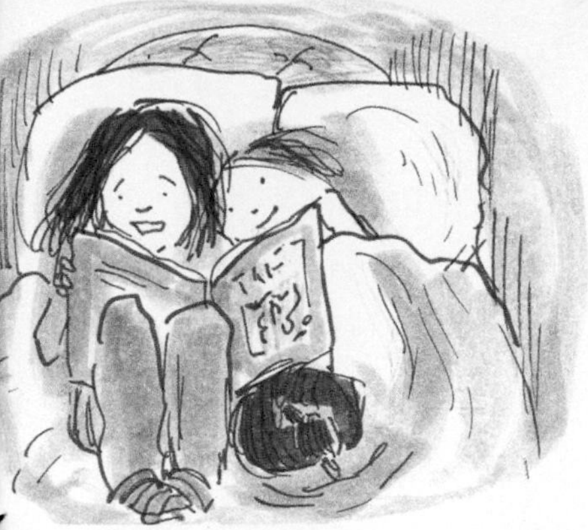

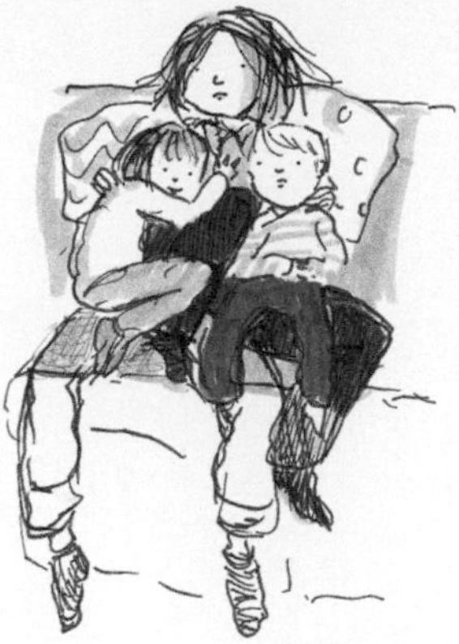

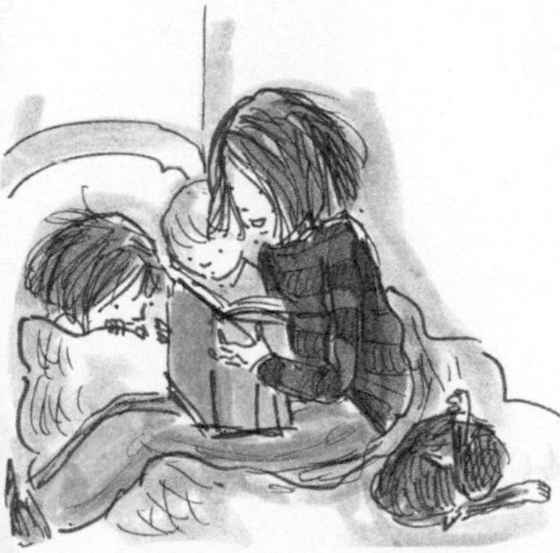

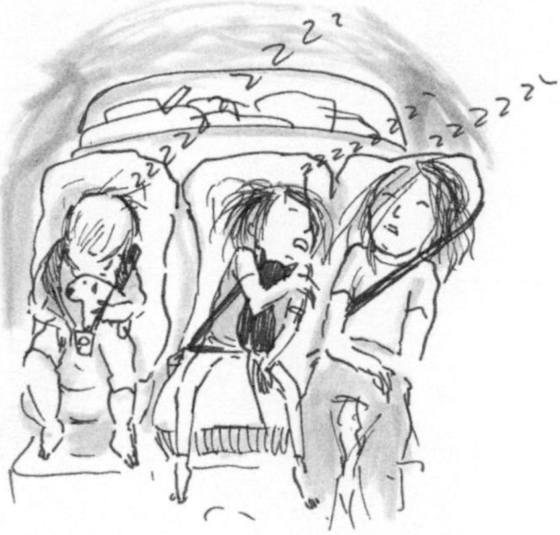

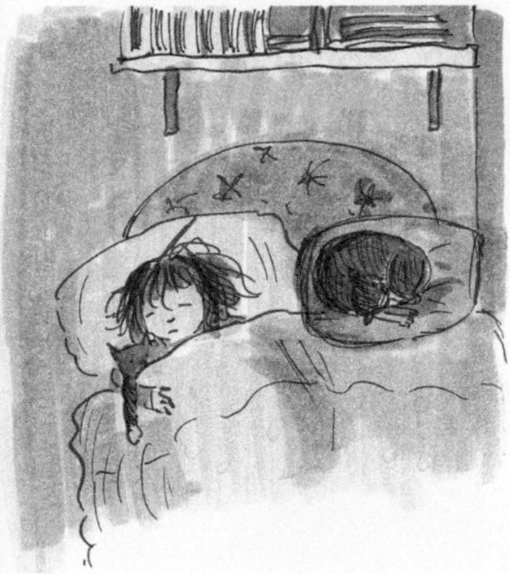

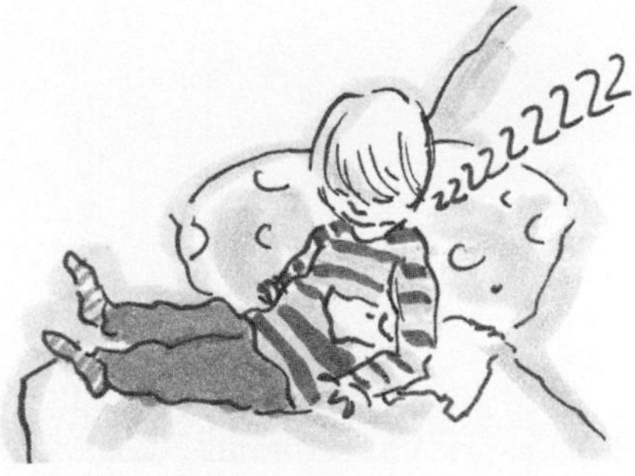

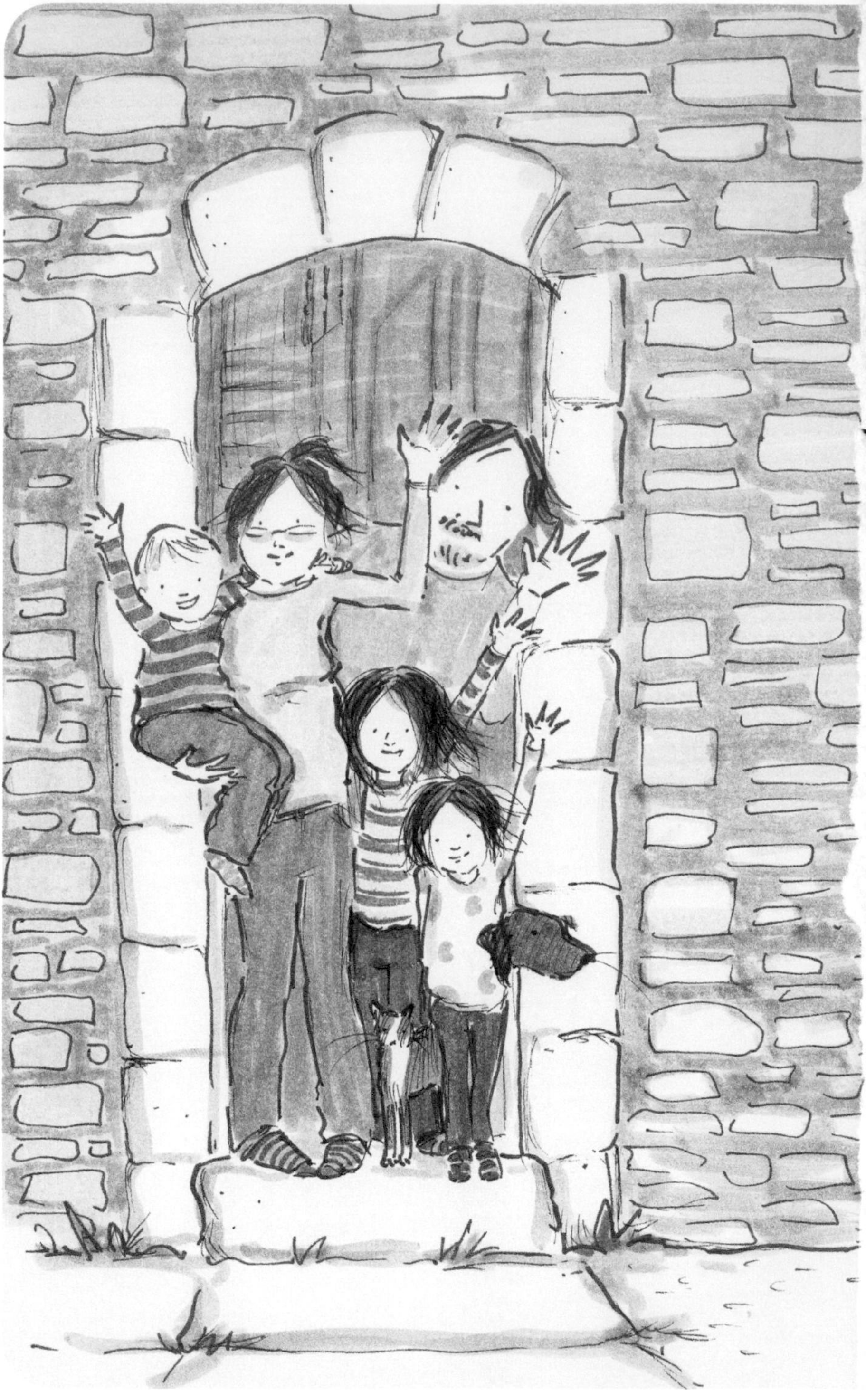

Goodbye! Come back soon!

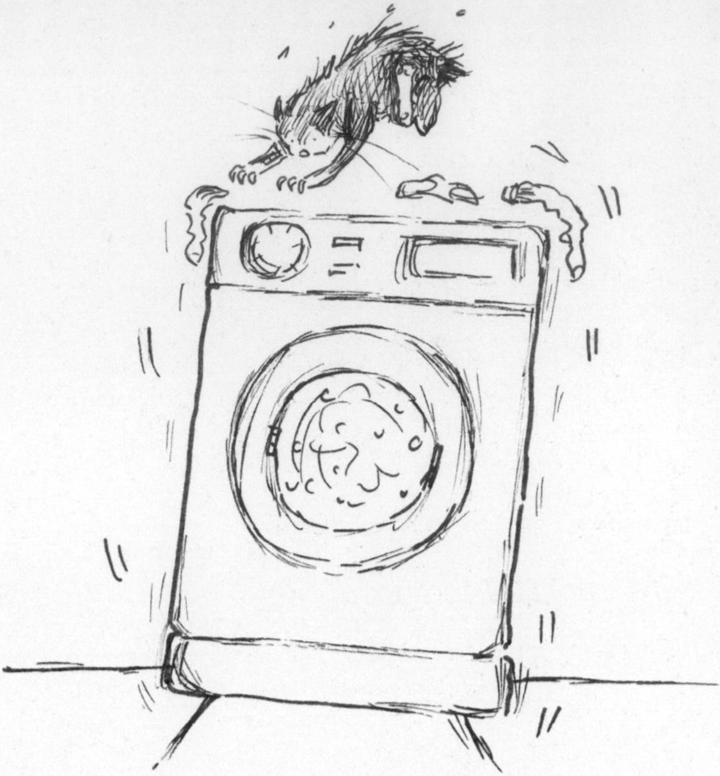

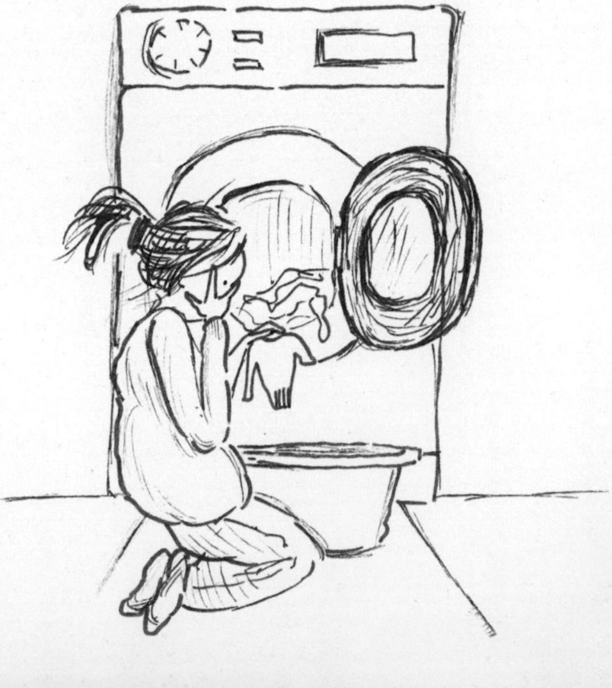